Exploring Unitarian Universalist Identity

Published by
RED BARN PUBLISHING
22 Mechanic Street
Rockland, ME 04841–3514

Library of Congress Control Number:

ISBN-10: 0-9741152-1-5
ISBN-13: 978-0-9741152-1-4

Book and cover design by • Amy Fischer Design, Camden, ME
Chalice icon designed by • Rev. Micha Lagueux, Richmond, ME
Printed and bound by • Berryville Graphics, Inc., Berryville, VA

FRONTISPIECE: First Church in Roxbury, fifth meeting house, 1804, John Eliot Square.

Exploring Unitarian Universalist Identity

THE MINNS LECTURES *for* 2005
"The Boston Religion: Special Themes"

by Peter Tufts Richardson

RED BARN PUBLISHING
Rockland, Maine

Contents

.

TO

My Grandchildren

Charles, Vann, Sarah, Peter and Sam

May their journeys on the planet be sustained in their human spiritual inheritance to which they may uniquely add their portion.

Preface

THE BOSTON RELIGION MARKED 375 YEARS of continuous worship in 2005. I wondered how a visitor to one of our congregations might relate when presented with this fact. Would they stare incredulously? Would they feel connected or disconnected? Would they wonder how one could care, as if history presented them with some kind of poison and their task is to find an antidote?

There is indeed a paradox in our existence, that the old Puritans could have morphed into something as radical as latter day Unitarianism and Unitarian Universalist practice. I have lived this paradox of history flowing irresistibly toward a global religious embrace. In my youth I first experienced Unitarian worship when the sermon that morning was vintage Emerson. I had just read his essay *On Self-Reliance* leaving my Protestant safe harbor for spiritual adventure.

It was an honor to give the 2005 Minns Lectures in celebration of the 375th anniversary of the First Church in Boston. My task was to take out of these $42^{1/2}$ decades what I believe to be the several most critical themes as we prepare for the century just entered. What can we learn from 375 years of experience of greatest benefit for congregations and their leaders? The lectures (1- 4) attempted: (1) to find our ground, whatever else defines us, as our starting place; (2) to define our polity in three historic models, giving us perspective and focus for structuring our congregational communities; (3) to define our intellectual center in the Transcendentalist revolt with the continuing presence Emerson provides for us, a rudder guiding our theological enterprise; and (4) to find a wider vision capable of holding multifarious energies of our religion for a ministry to the world as it is emerging in this century.

This volume aims to illumine our present Unitarian Universalist complex from the rich inheritance of our history. Perhaps you will resonate with these explorations or be moved to develop your own.

—Peter Tufts Richardson
November 21, 2005

The history of the church proves, that men may trust their faculties too little as well as too much, and that the timidity, which shrinks from investigation, has injured the mind, and betrayed the interests of Christianity as much as an irreverent boldness of thought.

—William Ellery Channing, 1809[1]

Overview: Finding Our Ground

WE SEEM NOT ONLY TO CONFUSE others but also ourselves in attempting to answer the question, what kind of religion is this? It seems to me one of the best ways to access answers to this question will be to look at our history in Boston. In the struggles of congregations and theologians to work through the great issues of each generation, in the daily work of congregational life and in the networks of relationship among congregations, ministers, and laity, we can gain insights into our uniqueness and emergence as Unitarians and now Unitarian Universalists.

We were, first and foremost, inheritors of the Puritan order. This was true in the structures of organization, congregational polity; in our theological orientation, trusting reason in interpreting scripture; and in our social responsibility. Unitarian ministers, for example, until 1833 were agents of the state, responsible for the moral, spiritual, intellectual well being of society. And after 1833 this sense of responsibility continued even if no longer officially sanctioned. And since we are speaking of Boston, with Harvard just across the river, with a dominance of commerce from the port of Boston and the largest population in New England, Boston was the cultural, social and intellectual head of the Puritan body.[3] If you held a Boston pulpit you had the ear of the entire Puritan system.

There was one exception to this generalization, of course, King's Chapel. Not of the Puritan order but rather of the Anglican order, it played a unique role. The church of the royal governors since they were first appointed in 1686, this Anglican presence in their midst forced the Puritan establishment to negotiate a religious toleration with the King in self defense. Otherwise it was not a foregone conclusion that the Puritan churches would have developed a climate of religious tolerance in New England. Secondly, there was a liberal Arminian wing of Anglicanism in England thus making King's Chapel a port of entry, if you will, of more liberal and enlightened ideas. While not the only way these ideas came into New England, we know they were rather concentrated in Boston. King's Chapel became Unitarian in the closing decades of the eighteenth century, one of the first to openly do so.[4]

During the Great Awakening in the colonies, evangelists came to Boston in three waves. The first in 1740 was met with great enthusiasm. Nearly everyone turned out to hear the evangelist, George Whitefield. The third wave a few years later met with a general indifference. What had changed? Charles Chauncy of the First Church was concerned that itinerant preachers came and left, stirring up unrest in the churches but not staying around to put the pieces of religious community back together again. Chauncy therefore had some meetings with his brethren clergy and even got on his horse for some more rural visits. When he was through he had eastern Massachusetts pretty well resistant to the revivalist virus. Important for us in this process, the immune system of the same territory became less resistant to liberal and Arminian ideas. The pathway towards Unitarianism lay open before them.

A word about theological language; if you are reading about late eighteenth or early nineteenth century New England and you come across the term, "Liberal Christian," you have found the code words for those Arminians or Arians or Socinians who were on their way to what became known as Unitarians. Arminians, named for the Dutch theologian, Jacob Arminius, were those tending towards more openness, more tolerance, more dependence upon free will and less upon determinism (such as Calvinist predestination). They were more inclined to prefer reason over revelation. Arians, named for the fourth century church father, Arius, elevated Jesus above the merely human but subordinate to God. Socinians, named for the Polish theologian, Faustus Socinus, saw Jesus as entirely human in nature. The name, Unitarian, was given to us by our opponents who lumped all these non-Trinitarian variations together, and with Jedediah Morse, asked the question, "Shall we have the Boston Religion or the Christian Religion?"[5] The Unitarians for the most part did not see themselves as a separate sect, but rather as the rational fulfillment of New England religious continuity.

When the dust finally settled, after 1805 and pretty much by 1825, what did "the Boston Religion" look like? In 1805 a Unitarian, Henry Ware, Sr., was appointed to the Hollis chair of Divinity at Harvard. Eight of the original nine Puritan churches in Boston, plus King's Chapel, had become Unitarian, making Unitarianism a majority religion. Unitarians held a virtual monopoly for those in jurisprudence, in political, commercial, educational, cultural, social and theological circles in the city and in surrounding eastern Massachusetts towns.

To give one example, we can look at those who founded the Boston Athenaeum. Unitarian ministers led by Joseph Stephens Buckminster, minister of the Brattle Square Church, convened the Anthology Society which published the first literary magazine in America, *The North American Review*. This society organized the Boston Athenaeum, the first library in Boston, and a major reason the city was called the "Athens of America." Of the ten incorporators four were Unitarian ministers and of the remaining six perhaps five were Unitarian laity.[6] Likewise Jeremy Belknap, minister of the Federal Street Church, is credited with founding the Massachusetts Historical Society. Nearly every charitable institution in the city was founded and financed by Unitarians in an age when government played a minor role in providing a safety net. For example, Perkins Institute for the Blind was financed by a merchant in Channing's Federal Street Church, Thomas Handasyd Perkins, and directed by Unitarians Samuel Gridley and Julia Ward Howe.

When Massachusetts disestablished the "standing order" of churches in 1833 there was no overnight change in attitude and focus by ministers and laity alike in the Unitarian churches of Boston and eastern Massachusetts. They still felt responsible for social morality and general spiritual wellbeing. Much of this energy was channeled into a movement for universal public education. In some ways it began in Channing's study. While non-sectarian, the schools as conceived by Unitarian Horace Mann and those around him focused upon the development of traditional moral and spiritual values as their first priority. Likewise for the chapel ministries of the Benevolent Fraternity of Unitarian Churches (now the UU Urban Ministry) and of the Warren Street Chapel, their mission was the inculcation of moral and spiritual values, "salvation by character."[7]

A phenomenon associated with being the establishment is the tendency of others to desire to be in close proximity. We can see this in numerous New England mill towns where middle managers and supervisors attended the church of the mill owners, which more often than not was Unitarian. Thus the Boston Unitarian churches were built large to accommodate the neighboring families that could afford to buy pews in them. The size of a meeting house was determined by the number of pews to be owned not by the anticipated attendance on Sunday mornings, an historical reality that might be reassuring to preachers today who see vast spaces of emptiness before them. Unitarians generally built buildings in the latest fashion and often spared little expense, which turned out to be a mixed blessing.

I filled *The Boston Religion* with pictures of these buildings which represent not only New England ecclesiastical architecture[8] but also the central importance of Unitarians in the cultural, social, and theological history of the city. (At this point 80 slides were shown.[9])

To summarize the statistics of Unitarianism in Boston, in 1800 there were 16 churches in the city, 9 of them Unitarian, 2 Baptist, 2 Episcopal, and one each Trinitarian Congregational, Universalist, and Methodist. While we have organized 74 churches in Boston at one time or another, Unitarians reached their peak in 1866 with 38 active Unitarian churches in the city.[10] Difficulties with maintaining a Unitarian hegemony however surfaced well before the post Civil War period. Imagine a congregation with the minister either opposing or supporting the Fugitive Slave Law when he had before him in the congregation judges and lawyers pledged to support it or defending those opposed to it, abolitionists making speeches in Faneuil Hall and leading demonstrations, mill owners and trading merchants importing cotton from the South, politicians hoping to stay in office, and people seeking solace or comfort who wished to hold the whole issue in abeyance. Then with the Civil War itself the sons of Unitarian families went off to war, often on horseback leading troops and therefore prime targets. Such divisions do not heal easily. After the abolition of slavery was resolved of course we immediately set about wrestling with the issue of women's suffrage. Our churches were not tranquil places of retreat from the everyday world. Add to social issues of the day, the great theological debates, the "miracles controversy" brought in by George Ripley, Theodore Parker and others, the introduction of "higher criticism" of the Bible by leading Transcendentalists, then the advent of Darwinian evolution, an orientation not to be found in the Bible. Those more inclined to quietism silently slipped away into Episcopalian environs which gradually became a fine place to be seen for the upwardly mobile.[11]

Or look at those who may have experienced financial reverses in their lives. If it became hard to pay the higher pew assessments in the fashionable Unitarian churches perhaps it was not so traumatic to find a pew in the lower rent district of the evangelicals and Universalists.[12] When you are on the top of the heap ecclesiastically in a city, you are sometimes the last to notice the gradual ebbing away of your demographic base. The demise of the Brattle Square Church in the Back Bay by 1882 sent shock waves of new awareness for the Unitarians.[13] This is the congregation about which Emerson wrote in his journals, "Boston or Brattle Street Christianity is a compound of force, or the best Diagonal line that can be drawn between Jesus Christ and Abbott Lawrence."[14]

Even so, when the Social Register began publication in Boston in 1890 of the 15 ministers listed, 12 were Unitarians, one was Episcopal and two were unknown (to the author).[15] Early in Boston's history some began to call the town a "preacher's paradise." It is hard to know when that designation waned and went out of useage, very likely by the turn of the twentieth century.[16] Among the oldest congregations only King's Chapel survived in its original neighborhood. Others stampeded into the Back Bay occupying corners on Arlington, Berkeley, Clarendon, and Exeter streets as well as Copley Square between Clarendon and Dartmouth. Of these only Arlington Street Church and First Church have survived. Certain of the outlying neighborhoods were prosperous for awhile—Dorchester, Jamaica Plain, West Roxbury. In 1900 there were 20 Unitarian churches in the city. Today there are seven. It has been said of James DeNormandie, for many years the distinguished minister of the First Church in Roxbury, that he had parishioners in every town in Massachusetts except Roxbury!

Much of the decline in the twentieth century was rooted in long-standing causes. In the late 1840s there was a massive immigration from Ireland caused by the potato famine there, increasing the population of Boston by a third overnight. There were few potential Unitarians among them for several generations. Whole neighborhoods around Unitarian churches filled with Roman Catholic immigrants, turning Federal mansions into tenement houses. Unitarians rarely engaged in city-wide planning. Congregations were formed from the initiative of people living in the neighborhoods. In addition by the mid-twentieth century the work of the UU Urban ministry shifted and the neighborhood chapel idea was phased out. Large sections of the city lost any Unitarian presence. I have mentioned pew ownership. Some churches did not phase out this method of church financing until well into the twentieth century, Arlington Street Church, for example, in 1935. This church had a controversy in the 1880s over empty pews when there was standing room only all around them, their owners absent, perhaps sailing off Nahant on a sunny Sunday. Charles Dole in Jamaica Plain complained, "you had no right in your church to seat a stranger in your neighbor's pew!"[17] Since churches were financed with pew assessments, Unitarians were slow to realize how critical to ministry in urban centers is the acquisition of hefty endowment funds. Without them churches go into a survival mode, repairing their buildings, paying a minister, but not staffing for outreach and programming for the diverse needs and aspirations of urban dwellers.

There have been exceptions to the general pattern of retrenchment. Several times theater preaching has caught hold involving large numbers. Theodore Parker was the pioneer, preaching in the Melodeon, then the Music Hall, from 1845 to 1859. Congregations numbered 2500 each week and his church numbered 7000 members. After his death they remained in the Music Hall another three years until falling back to smaller halls. Shortly after this when the New North Church and the Bulfinch Street Church were on their last legs they merged, sold their buildings, and migrated to the Music Hall with the leadership and preaching of the latter-day Transcendentalist, William Roundsville Alger. For four years they regularly drew congregations upwards of two thousand until Alger left them in 1873 and the whole arrangement collapsed. A third congregation involving large numbers was the Community Church which at its peak rented Symphony Hall each week, from 1927 to 1942. There were numerous guest preachers, some filling it to its 2600 person capacity. It should be asked if these ventures reflected "liberal" times in society, and whether in general they helped or hurt the fortunes of the larger Unitarian movement.

Whether it be theater preaching or the general health of the Unitarian body, we need to attend both to the milieu in which we work and the internal orientation and vision which inspires us. Unitarianism in Boston and coastal New England grew its strength from a maritime base. There is a certain openness, a restlessness, a larger embrace among populations oriented to global trading. Awareness of Arabic, Indian or Chinese influences broadens one's comprehension beyond the fencerows and forested hills of one's immediate landscape. A certain confidence builds with the capacity to outfit global voyages, time appearances in far-away markets, manage the sustenance and survival of crews and ships for long-distance travel over the horizon from home port (all this long before the invention of the radio). Cosmopolitan awareness and confidence in individual judgment entered into the meeting house mix when Unitarianism was fermenting in coastal congregations.

Even as the Unitarian controversy was fading into the second quarter of the nineteenth century, the economic base was shifting from a maritime to an industrial orientation. By mid-century, Boston bankers and financiers were investing more in textile mills and later in railroads than in ships and cargos. A different kind of attentiveness enters into the managing of mills, the movement of raw materials, manufacturing machines, exploitation of a large labor force in a local mill. We see this same shift from the elegant Federal style homes of ship owners to the heavy-set brownstone row houses of later financiers. The earlier homes were filled with light and simply furnished. The Back Bay on the other hand specialized in dark interiors, with heavy draperies and Gothic décor. Likewise church architecture shifted from clear windowed, image free, clarity of features, to heavy Romanesque and Gothic stone, with stained glass, thick carpets, ornate carved woodwork. Liturgically as well, taste and sentiment shifted from a Puritan simplicity focused in the spoken word with lined-out hymns, to an Anglican aesthetic with professional choirs, robed clergy and liturgists, and service books resembling the Book of Common Prayer. Several ministers and many more laity eventually jumped ship and joined the Episcopalians.[18] One of these, Frederick Dan Huntington, shortly after taking up the priesthood, wrote James Freeman Clarke a letter dated, "Friday, St. Barnabas Day" to which Clarke replied with a letter dated, "Monday, Wash Day." Differences between congregations became so subtle, some distinguished Episcopalians from Unitarians by noting whether they kneeled in church or bowed in slight deference.

One benefit of an historical perspective on our religion is a release from the public relations and numbers crunching mentality which is pervasive in American society today. A certain generosity comes into play when we can place ourselves into perspective. It is highly probable we will never be a majority religion again. But as Kenneth Patton once said, "your value is in your quality, not in your bulk."[19] It becomes important to let that go, to become who we truly are in this time.[20]

So far we have described something of the characteristics of the Boston Religion. In images and words we have portrayed the unique qualities of this religion not only in Boston but for American culture as well. Sometimes visitors come through the doors and ask, "What do Unitarian Universalists believe?" For us this is an awkward question, really the wrong question.[21] We know who we are, for the many experiences of the last 375 years have formed a continuity of connection that is us. Theologically of course we have many layers.[22] As already emphasized we are the inheritors of the Puritan legacy. We still have the darkest robes in interfaith processions! We actually believe that reason is an instrument and guide in the religious life. We see as an integral part of our orientation a sense of responsibility for the spiritual wellbeing of society. But we are more than latter day Puritans. With Channing and his generation we have a confidence in human nature, that the human mind, the human conscience, the human capacity to live generously in love, is in kinship at the deepest levels in a spiritual connection which he called God. We seek to empower the individual, for Channing the sole reason for human institutions including the church, and summarized in Emerson's great essay, *Self-Reliance*. The individual in a developing capacity to understand, to embrace the world, to become a deeper spiritual being, is the foundation of congregational life and human aspiration. With Emerson we aim to be representative, above any single generation with its transient fashions and expectations, to be for our times its poet-prophets.[23] And we set no bounds on our love, we seek to embrace the whole of our human inheritance, to erect no arbitrary barriers of ideology or cultural determinism, to be citizens of this time, this world, and this congregation.

It is not easy to call up the images of this continuity. It takes some immersion in history. In the eighteenth century Charles Chauncy was our center. Everything, it seemed, was referenced around "Charles, Old Brick."[24] In the nineteenth century Channing was our spiritual genius, always ghostlike present. With whatever machinations life presented us, Channing stabilized, reassured, even as a wounded healer, a profound presence. Emerson's journey out to Concord, his meditations in nature, in deep direct connection with spiritual power, in the poetic singing of the pervasive human sustenance, he is always the corrective to myopic busyness. He became our reference point, his image merging in every New England landscape, every American philosophy, every world perspective, "the oracles of Concord."[25] He becomes a Unitarian archetype. Chauncy,[26] Channing and Emerson lived a long time ago, and yet they have a continuing reality for us, in all our diversity. That no major endearing figures have since appeared does not leave us confused or wholly bereft for they are with us. Who today is our spiritual guide? What now is our vision? We shall address this question in the next three chapters. But Chauncy, Channing, Emerson will never leave us, even now.

*Liberalism is the supreme form of generosity; it is the right
which the majority concedes to minorities and hence it is
the noblest cry that has ever resounded in this planet.
It announces the determination to share existence with the
enemy; more than that, with an enemy which is weak.
It was incredible that the human species should have
arrived at so noble an attitude, so paradoxical, so refined,
so acrobatic, so antinatural. Hence, it is not to be wondered
at that this same humanity should soon appear anxious to
get rid of it. It is a discipline too difficult and complex to
take firm root on earth.*

—José Ortega y Gasset, *The Revolt of the Masses*[1]

CHAPTER TWO

Congregational Life: Standing Order, Free Association, Pluralism

LET US EXAMINE THE BASIS for congregational life in light of three different social orientations: (1) an organic model, of Unitarianism as the established religion in Massachusetts; (2) a volunteristic or autonomous model, based in philosophies of natural rights and individual liberties; and (3) a pluralistic model, based in a matured liberal philosophy. Around discussion of these three models for congregational life we will bring in relevant changes in the social context, and consider what these changes have meant for ministers and members in Unitarian congregations in Boston and in general to the present day.

We first examine an organic model, what it was like for Unitarians to be the established religion, or as it was called the Standing Order. In the Unitarian Controversy, beginning about 1805, the state religion in Massachusetts supported by local taxation split along theological lines into the Unitarian Congregational and Trinitarian Congregational churches. In the larger towns with multiple churches, instead of taxation on the property owners, taxes were levied on the pew owners for support of the minister and the meeting house. As we saw in Chapter One, eight of the nine congregational churches of the Standing Order in Boston became Unitarian by 1805: First Church, Old North Church, Brattle Square Church, New North Church, New South Church, Federal Street Church, Hollis Street Church and the West Church. Only Old South Church opted to take the Trinitarian Congregational alternative. In addition, King's Chapel, New England's oldest Episcopal Church, became Unitarian in 1784. Thus at the beginning of the nineteenth century Unitarians were a majority as well as the established religion in the city. To understand the significance of this it will be helpful to picture the Boston Religion in its context of the Puritan landscape of Massachusetts Bay.

The multitudes who visit New England today often are attracted by a charm only dimly understood. Somehow the picture of colonial and federal houses clustered together with a classic revival or wooden gothic church in its center, draws into consciousness a dimly remembered past, a time long ago when life and society were integrated in one whole, where the life of the town and the life of the individual resonated in one pulse, one life. It is of course the medieval model, transplanted here, where the people lived clustered together surrounded by their farmlands. They were born into the parish and died from it. If a person were strongly attracted into a spiritual orientation they joined the church and were admitted into communion. The community of the church was the parish of the entire surrounding village. The landscape supported a communal integrity and if a member found themself in a neighboring village, they felt at home there as well because the language of the familiar order in the fields, homes and village could be read.

In place of an Anglican Church in the center as they had experienced back home in England they instituted their own congregationally governed parishes. Indeed, the legislature of the Commonwealth stipulated that a town could not be organized and incorporated unless it supported a church and ministry in its midst. This was an organic model of society with its church in the center.

Critical for shaping this form of religion at the center was the Church of the Pilgrims. The Plymouth Colony preceded Massachusetts Bay by nine years. Plymouth had been founded intact, carrying over from England (and Holland) their original covenant from Scrooby. It read as follows:

> We, the Lord's free people, have joined ourselves into a
> church estate, in the fellowship of the gospel, to walke in all
> his wayes, made known or to be made known, according to
> our best endeavors, whatsoever it should cost us, the Lord
> assisting us.[2]

This simple language places the people in community as the central reality, living together as best they could in the way set forth in the Gospels and developed through their experience. When the Puritans to the north landed in Salem in 1629 Plymouth sent their Deacon, Samuel Fuller, to influence the institution of a like simplicity there, without elaborate and divisive doctrinal distinctions. Jettisoned as well was the idea of using the English prayer book. From the beginning New England would have nothing between the gospel and congregational experience, no creeds, no liturgical books, no images, not even flowers on the communion table or pulpit. Focus upon life together in the here and now with the absence of divisive creedal affirmations was essential for the continuity a century and a half later into an Arminian and then Unitarian orientation in the old parishes. The covenantal relationship was embracing and parish-wide.[3]

The success of the Puritan Commonwealth was phenomenal as might be expected in a largely unexploited landscape together with an ethic of hard work. Aside from the hardships of New England's winters, generous supplies of glacial stones and the occasional terror of Indian raids in the colonial wars, the New England countryside was remarkably uniform in concept. Massachusetts Bay held a vision of society "as a light to the nations" in a context of Divine Providence.[4]

It is axiomatic that every body needs a head[5] and Boston from 1630 onwards formed the core and vision for the whole body of Puritan churches. The Plymouth Colony dissolved into Massachusetts Bay in 1692. The District of Maine was a part of Massachusetts until 1820. New Hampshire, a separate colony, was networked religiously with the Puritan establishment. In the two generations of Arminian development leading to the Unitarian Controversy in 1805 and following, the Boston churches provided the decisive playing field. As recently as the funeral of Adlai Stevenson in 1965 his mother was referred to by news commentators as "of the Boston Unitarian religion."[6]

Imagine New England religion without leadership from such as John Wilson and John Cotton of the First Church, Increase and Cotton Mather of the Old North Church, Jonathan Mayhew of the West Church, Charles Chauncy again of First Church, or Jeremy Belknap and William Ellery Channing of the Federal Street Church! And after 1825 with the organization of the American Unitarian Association try to imagine our history without Henry Ware Jr. of Old North/Second Church, Ezra Stiles Gannett of the Arlington Street Church, Joseph Tuckerman of the Friend Street Chapel, John Pierpont and Thomas Starr King of the Hollis Street Church, George Ripley of the Thirteenth Congregational Church and Brook Farm, Theodore Parker of the Twenty-Eighth Congregational Society, James Freeman Clarke of the Church of the Disciples, Minot Savage of the Church of the Unity, or Edward Everett Hale of South Congregational Church. Not only did Boston ministers give leadership but Boston merchants, educators and literary figures provided a massive financial and cultural influence. When historian, Ann Douglas, in *The Feminization of American Culture* called Unitarians the "established among the established" she doubtless had in mind the Unitarian hegemony in Boston.[7]

A typical Sunday in most Massachusetts parishes consisted in a morning and an afternoon worship service for which the minister prepared two sermons. About half the time ministers engaged in exchanges with neighboring colleagues in order to lighten the burden of preparation. Congregations treasured this tradition for it gave them benefit of various perspectives, theological and exegetical. Together with advisory multi-parish counsels formed for ordinations and called for consultations in times of local crisis, pulpit exchanges kept village and city churches from becoming insular. We see for example as the tendency away from Calvinism towards Arminianism developed, congregations tended to be well informed even to the fine points of theological distinctions. When the Unitarian controversy finally broke out at the turn of the nineteenth century more often than not a congregation already knew where it was on the theological spectrum and largely came over to one side or the other as a body with few dissenters removing themselves. For example, before their annexation into the city of Boston the three churches in Roxbury (now Roxbury, Jamaica Plain, and West Roxbury) transitioned to Unitarianism without schisms and remained the only churches in their towns until their populations increased. In Roxbury the Universalists and Baptists organized in 1820, in Jamaica Plain the Baptists organized in 1840 and Episcopalians in 1841, and in West Roxbury the Orthodox Congregationalists eventually organized a separate church.

Socially a church functioned as the focus of a town, where people routinely touched base as a part of their life together. There needed to be no separate groups in a congregation to heighten social relationships for most members spent their lifetimes together. In the whole context of the town when there was a house or barn fire the town bell in the church steeple called the alarm. When a town meeting or national political event required a meeting it was held in the church. In the mid-nineteenth century when Henry David Thoreau was gliding down the Concord River he heard the church bell, and reflected upon how it centered the lives of all within range of its sound, even himself.[8] The First Parish Unitarian of course was the church he stayed away from. So far as we know other churches in town were not in the running for this honor!

Pews in the churches of course were bought and sold like real estate. The aim of church architecture was not to build for the size of anticipated attendance, but to build so that families who wished to purchase a pew could be accommodated. Seldom would every pew be filled on the same Sunday and no expectation existed that a minister fill the room. Often the only organization associated with the church was the Proprietors, a group of men who owned the pews, overseeing repairs of the meeting house, use of the building, and paying of the minister(s) and sexton.

A central consideration of ministers in the Standing Order was to monitor and engage in teaching to lift the moral and spiritual wellbeing of all. Not only in preaching but in parish calling and participating in community networks of organization such as existed, this was critical for the ministerial role. In larger parishes a second and usually younger minister was often called the "teacher." When the town instituted a separate school house for its children usually it was the minister who superintended its work, and often a student for divinity at Harvard was employed to work directly with the children. Religion thus fulfilled its traditional role in transmitting cultural values to each succeeding generation.

Moving from the landscapes of rural New England to the larger cities this picture was translated into neighborhood churches, each holding pews belonging to surrounding families. There was no need for a signboard on the church for everyone knew what it was, the church for all within a half mile or so who could afford to buy a pew. But it was really a church responsible for the well being of all within sound of its bell. For Unitarians this orientation continued long after disestablishment in 1833. As late as 1885 Brooke Herford minister of the Arlington Street Church complained that only rarely did the Unitarian churches of the city have even a sign board on their buildings.[9]

By 1833 then, Unitarians had inherited about one third of the established parishes in Massachusetts. Their ministers were state as well as parish officers responsible for monitoring and addressing the moral and spiritual wellbeing of their geographical parishes. When Massachusetts disestablished religion in 1833 Unitarians found themselves thrown back on their own voluntaristic base. In their behavior however, the ministers and leading laymen continued much as before in their attitudes and sense of responsibility for the society around them, even to the extent of neglecting to build up institutions to sustain a sectarian existence, for example, endowments, sign boards, sectarian schools or strategic planning for growing new and old congregations. This organic vision and inertia for the Unitarian order, much the same as the now disestablished Standing Order, continued at the center of the Unitarian orientation for another half century and more. Thus we have Harvard President Kirkland's designation of Unitarians as "the unsectarian sect" and Douglas's characterization of Unitarians as the "established among the established," continuing long after this perspective was helpful either for growth or for vitality of the movement.[10]

There was, however, a second and contrasting tradition to the organic one of the Standing Order. I am calling it a volunteristic or autonomous model where congregations depend upon the individuals who sell their pew in their neighborhood church and choose to purchase another regardless of location in order to affiliate with a particular church. Dating from well before the Revolutionary War the Arminian development, influenced by the English empiricists, pioneered in New England by such as Charles Chauncy of the First Church and Jonathan Mayhew of the West Church,[11] developed a view of natural rights and individual liberty. This alternative, beginning in the mid eighteenth century in Boston, eventually rescued Unitarians from the inertias of the older organic model.

The organic model of the establishment was grounded in territorial parishes, the church and its minister served the people of a certain town or neighborhood. Only gradually did some respond to the newer model of choosing affiliation with a church for non geographical or sectarian reasons. While ministers were known for different views and abilities, only with time did the unique characteristics of a congregation pose a reason for joining. Brattle Square and First Church were known for their social prestige, West Church for its radical independence, Federal Street for Channing's presence, for example. All Boston's Unitarian churches sold and taxed pews like real estate for their maintenance.

In the order of things we were born with certain unalienable rights which it was our duty to exercise to the best of our ability and free judgment in family, church and society. This is why the Arminian generation warned of the danger of an English imposition of an Anglican bishop in New England. While this was avoided both Mayhew and Chauncy feared a bishop together with the royal governors would set up a collusion directly threatening to the religious Standing Order and American liberties. Ecclesiastical authority in a hierarchy was diametrically opposed to the New England system but increasingly even more important, opposed to authority placed in individuals themselves. This had been the basis of John Locke's influential argument in his 1689 *Letter Concerning Toleration*:

> ...all churches were obliged to lay down toleration as the
> foundation of their own liberty; and teach that liberty of
> conscience is every man's natural right, equally belonging
> to dissenters as to themselves; and that nobody ought to be
> compelled in matters of religion either by law or force.[12]

By the time William Ellery Channing preached his Baltimore Sermon in 1819 and his subsequent critiques of Calvinism, reliance on individual autonomy in matters of belief and practice as the basis for congregational life was becoming well established. There was increasing shifting around of pew ownership among the churches of Boston, a pattern beginning in Mayhew's time. One of the reasons given for Old South's remaining with the orthodox side of the Unitarian controversy was the number of pew owners who had shifted their allegiance over to Channing's Federal Street Church. Even out in the country where a town would contain only one church, the religious views tended to cluster around one theological tendency, orthodox or liberal, sometimes despite those the minister happened to hold. For example in the old Pilgrim church in Plymouth, the minister for 39 years was Chandler Robbins, so orthodox he wrote a creed to keep things defined. Upon his death in 1799 the congregation called James Kendall, an avowed Liberal Christian, as the Unitarians were then calling themselves.

The New England mind was opening, beyond the local town, even beyond the provincial capital, to embrace the world. Entrepreneurial merchants in Salem and Boston were now sending ships not only to Europe, but to Arab capitals in the Mediterranean, ports in Africa and the Caribbean, and around the horn and South America to California and the Northwest and even to India and China. It was a global embrace. At minimum a new confidence in human resourcefulness and competence came into everyday assumptions and expectations. This confidence in human nature entered the churches, particularly east of Worcester and along the coast from Eastport, ME, to Newport, RI, seeding outposts in Providence, New York, Philadelphia, Baltimore, Charleston, Savannah, New Orleans, San Francisco.

The great theologian of the Unitarian reappraisal of human nature, replacing Calvinist views of innate depravity and predestination by a despotic

God, was William Ellery Channing. We are called to expand into our potential as free beings, progressively resonating with the Divine presence opening within us, responding from an enlivened conscience within to the moral order pervading the universe. In his sermon, "Spiritual Freedom," in 1830 Channing gives a stirring litany of ten characteristics of the free mind[13] followed by a summary of the purpose of free institutions:

> The chief benefit of free institutions is clear and
> unutterably precious. Their chief benefit is, that they aid
> freedom of mind, that they give scope to man's faculties,
> that they throw him on his own resources, and summon
> him to work out his own happiness. It is, that, by removing
> restraint from intellect they favor force, originality, and
> enlargement of thought. It is, that, by removing restraint
> from worship, they favor the ascent of the soul to God.[14]

But for Channing to give as the purpose of free institutions, religious or civic, the growth of individual human potential, did not in any way cause him to disparage their importance. The previous year (1829) he had developed a pioneering study of voluntary associations clearly marking human nature as social and, for our purposes here, congregational life as empowering, as the generator for earnestness, energy, and strength, as a stimulation for the mind and creativity, and as a medium for the individual exercise of freedom. Intellectual and moral progress are sustained and while judgment is reserved for the individual, entering into voluntary association can accomplish more than an individual could hope for alone. And he warns against religious imposition of uniformity and the impression of large numbers which can lure us into the grip of tyrannies over our moral and intellectual faculties.[15]

We see in Channing quite remarkably that while he had advocated continuance of the system of a religious establishment and had seen his own ministry centrally focused in that model, at the same time well before 1833 he marked out the parameters of religious congregations as voluntary associations of individuals. Neither Channing nor others in his generation moved beyond this point to a resolution. The leading pioneers for bringing congregational life to a full voluntary association were James Freeman Clarke and his Church of the Disciples.

In 1841 James Freeman Clarke founded the Church of the Disciples on a new basis, that the pews would be free and financial support placed upon a voluntary basis. In addition there would be group life in the congregation, study groups, advocacy groups for social reform, men's and women's organizations, social service and charitable enterprises. A third innovation was participation of laity in leading worship, even lay sermons. And of course the Church of the Disciples organized a Sunday School, as was becoming common at that time. It took a quarter century before The Church of the Disciples was viable and showed signs of strengthening to become one of Boston's leading Unitarian churches. Organizing so that creative initiatives of individuals marked the climate of congregational life thus took a full century to emerge after the model of natural rights and individual autonomy and responsibility was first preached from Arminian and Unitarian pulpits. The Church of the Disciples came to be nicknamed "The Catchall Church."[16]

That Channing was seen in attendance at the Church of the Disciples alongside his two brothers, is evidence of the progressive vision of the man. His colleague, Clarke, was creating something he knew his prosperous Federal Street Church would not consider. Arlington Street Church, successor to the Federal Street Church would not relinquish its pew ownerships until 1935 nor expand into group life resembling a modern day congregation until the ministry of Samuel Eliot in the third and fourth decades of the twentieth century. Channing's attendance at the Church of the Disciples can be seen as one of his greatest acts not only of generosity but of imagination. He could well have retreated to his study instead.[17]

Building the Church of the Disciples involved traumatic reversals threatening its survival. Its minister, James Freeman Clarke, was counted among the theological conservatives in the generation following Channing. But he also possessed a sense of fair play and inclusion towards those who differed. When most Unitarian ministers refused to exchange pulpits with the radical Transcendentalist, Theodore Parker, Clarke did exchange with him, not once but three times. This was more than sixteen families could countenance. They split off and built a large building on Bedford Street, The Church of the Saviour.[18]

Thus we encounter our third model of congregational life coming into being, leading to an eventual pluralistic orientation. Is it possible, not only in the movement generally, but also in an independent church, to have a pluralistic assemblage of individuals and groups, overlapping in their values and views, but not in a uniformity of agreement? To what extent need a congregation have an ideology or purpose to which every element within the congregation assents? To those who founded the Church of the Saviour the answer was yes. There must be a basic uniformity. But can we agree today?

For example, when the National Conference of Unitarian Churches was first organized in 1865 it was thought it might include liberal churches of many backgrounds. James Freeman Clarke, a proven fair minded Christian, gave the keynote speech, A member of his church, Governor Andrew, presided and Edward Everett Hale was elected as secretary. Delegates preferred the Unitarian name and proceeded to impose a boundary in the preamble of their new constitution, "disciples of the Lord Jesus Christ."While not a creed this simple phrase excluded a minority who were moving beyond this boundary while still connected with Unitarians in general. Those influenced by Parker's form of Transcendentalism, those inclined to broader affirmations than Christian only, those on the rationalist/scientific end of the spectrum, felt marginalized and went on to organize a separate Free Religious Association (FRA) in 1867. In addition several "conservative" congregations, mostly in Boston, did not join. An effort to embrace impulses beyond the mainstream of Unitarianism had failed. It remains an open question whether a wider base would have enhanced or detracted from the success of the Conference.

We do know the formation of the National Conference released a good deal of energy for revitalizing Unitarianism. The mainstream grew modestly for a time. The conservative congregations who boycotted the conference were wealthy and continued much as before. The radical wing organized their own FRA continuing their pioneering intellectual ferment which eventually leavened the larger movement. Thus breaking the stasis of the past several decades was more important than the wording of their constitution.

If we look at the last several decades of the twentieth century we may see a comparable pattern of being stuck. The now merged Unitarian Universalist Association (1961) seems to have settled into a kind of stasis or inertia without a clear sense of its place among the world's religious groupings or a strategic vision for a unique mission. What is our place in the whole picture which we might uniquely fill or fulfill? As opposed to being content to perpetuate whatever it is that we have been or are, in short, what will be our call to adventure?

To find an answer to this question it may be in order to explore a number of possibilities in parallel in an affirmation of pluralism in the movement as a whole and in our congregations. The signs of this alternative can already be seen in many places, but much of it is hit-or-miss and inadvertent rather than intentional.

Pluralism can be modeled in two aspects, as a process and as a philosophy. As a process it is fairly easy to see how a situation of pluralism can emerge largely before it is recognized as such in an open and liberal system. For example, the advent of feminism in our congregations spawned the Women In Religion movement, a changed gender-neutral language now universal among us and eventuated in a majority of women in the Unitarian Universalist ministry. Likewise, beginning with resolutions of witness in the 1980s, and the Welcoming Congregation program widely implemented in congregations, Unitarian Universalists have now asserted leadership in civil equality for gay, lesbian and transgendered persons in American society. Our congregations are largely hospitable and openly affirmative. Both developments began as minority perspectives in congregations with varying degrees of tolerance and support in the overall matrix of attention. By no means was it a forgone conclusion that either would receive the universal support they now enjoy.

Pluralism must work on the assumption that minorities may always be minorities but that some may emerge as major influences and even come to characterize the movement. We see in our congregations not only the traditional divergence of attention between the adult worshipping congregation and religious education programs, with subgroups such as choirs, creative worship committees, teacher training and religious education committees, but other programs which capture the primary attention and focus of many. A partial list may include small group ministry, young adult or "contemporary" worship, Buddhist or Yoga or Taoist meditation, a U.U. Christian circle, a neo pagan or earth based spirituality program (celebrating Celtic quarter and cross-quarter holidays), an annual Passover Seder and additional Jewish awareness activities, gatherings for interfaith families— usually before the winter holidays, ongoing groups for social service or social justice advocacy, as well as Welcoming Congregation and women's support activities. This is only a sampling.

For the first time in our history worship has become multi-focused in many places. No longer is one room and one time the central defining activity for a congregation. We must ask whether the preaching function and the free pulpit will endure as our leading characteristic. The rapid rise of small group ministries leads to the question, what calls them forth? In some congregations it may be a need to focus support for diversity. Small groups are a pluralism. In other congregations small groups appear to live at the interface of groups in an already existing pluralism. Face to face, relational, small groups may act as glue in a diverse congregational setting. In addition, the role of the minister enters the picture as supporter and interpreter of all, confidante and participant, yet engaged as minister of all, present in their own personal perspective.[19] Congregational leaders increasingly require a new non-anxious facility for managing a complexity of relationships, priorities, resources and strategic vision.[20] Engaging congregational life as itself a spiritual discipline may increasingly become intentional.

The pluralism model needs to be considered as a philosophy as well as a process. Pope John 23rd spoke of Catholic diversity as "unity in essentials, freedom in debatable matters, charity in everything." What may be the "unity in essentials" among Unitarian Universalists today? There is the Unitarian "one God" (perhaps deistic, perhaps personal, perhaps existential, perhaps as process, perhaps emergent or evolutionary, etc.), the pagan several "gods/goddesses," and some descendents of the Transcendentalists with God as in all or even "all is God." Perhaps instead of a common view of God it is human nature that is affirmed. But how? What does "the inherent worth and dignity of every person" actually mean for congregational life? Does it mean that we invite pedophiles, paranoid schizophrenics or just plain mean people into full congregational participation? Philosophically pluralism means we cannot reduce our "unity in essentials" to a monistic or dualistic principle. The world exists at a more complex level. But on the other hand pluralism is not equivalent with relativism. Some estimates of value and the good are better than others, and the differences can be acted upon. And some ideas of reality are less accurate than others. We do not inhabit a flat earth, for example, even though many people point "up" to heaven, teach plane geometry in schools and write poems about "sun sets" and "sun rises." Such notions are simply wrong. Were one of our churches to be captured by the Flat Earth Society they would still be wrong. So, too, we are capable of making judgments about the good life or human wellbeing and be more right than alternatives proffered. But I have still not identified our "unity in essentials." Thus we have one reason why, for now, we need an open pluralism for our congregational life.[21]

In a consumer-based society many visitors enter with a shopping list of needs and comforts they hope to have filled. The pastoral aspect of congregational life is essential but the central focus must be a challenge to spiritual growth. In a pluralistic congregation this is transmitted interactively either directly with the individual or indirectly in face to face groups. Philosophers and theologians from Channing to Jung have seen the growth of consciousness as our moral duty. A pluralistic congregation may confound the consumer of religion mentality because it is not a single mode environment. There may be a confusion of invitations to greet one at the door, shaking loose the product oriented expectations with a time for sorting and reflecting, shaking loose conventions and connecting with the self that is to grow. A multi centered congregation does not offer a mirror but rather engages the need for choice, to identify one's own path, to differentiate. A multi centered congregation engages at several levels, keeps one in the presence of alternatives and hones the congregation's capacity to serve a multi centered world.

Many, perhaps most, may perceive pluralism as a centripetal force. I caution that it can equally be seen as an exploratory force, providing much needed input for our ongoing continuity, very much a centrifugal process. Pluralism is interactive enlivening of congregational life and giving people with a wide diversity of backgrounds a place to land and a base for creative imagination and expression. Our congregations could become workshops for working out in religious community what we recommend and advocate in a wider diverse and pluralistic society and planetary humanity. The challenge in a pluralistic congregation, philosophically, will always be to hold it with a large enough vision.

I have discussed three models of congregational life, an organic or geographical model; a natural rights or individualist model; and a pluralistic model. As you might guess these models establish a foundation for the next two lectures. But here today there are two essential issues to raise by way of putting this discussion into historic context.

First, it may seem strange to you that I have not so far even mentioned the term, congregational polity. Historically it developed as a characteristic of the established churches in Massachusetts. There would be a good deal of consultation, pulpit exchanging, protecting of mutual interests in society, but every congregation was autonomous. Even when the ideology of natural rights and individual responsibility entered into New England discourse in the mid-eighteenth century, this form of church governance continued and remained central among Unitarians to the present day. However, it has gradually transformed in the second model to a radical form. Not only is the local church independent and participation voluntary but every member of that church is independently responsible for their own spiritual development and their own manner of participation. Such radical independence was virtually unknown in the collective consciousness of early New England congregational life. As this radical form of individualized polity relates to our emerging pluralism, the third model, it remains to be seen what meaning congregational polity may hold. It likely will involve resistance to pressures for conformity among congregations. In addition, much criticism of congregational life today confuses discomfort with individual autonomy with discomfort over the diversity of energies in an emerging pluralism.

Second, we must look at the cultural context in which our congregations exist and to which they minister. It seems to me it is critical to have in mind a strategic idea of the interface of one or more of these three models with the amazing historic transformations underway in world society. We live inside a world of epical change. As we anticipate patterns emergent in the twenty-first century it is critical that we examine how congregational life may interface with them.

It is generally acknowledged that we are experiencing the end of the modern age, problematical when we consider that American Unitarianism began well within the frame of Enlightenment modernity. Something different is finding its content and shape. Concepts such as "liberal" and "conservative" are becoming so cloudy as to be useless.[22] William Irwin Thompson emphasizes how the literate Enlightenment world is giving way to an electronic and noetic participatory milieu. Literature is fading before pictures, the alphabet before a new hieroglyphic way of thinking manifest in computer graphics and animation. Rather than a demythologized and abstract thought we have a new mythic and concrete mind emerging.[23]

Here are several indicators. In our time according to Edwin Friedman there is a failure of nerve, an overheated anxious society, inhibiting the emergence of well differentiated leaders.[24] Historian John Lukacs emphasizes, "at the end of an age intellectual consensus is almost always wrong."[25] Lee Harris further describes how intellectuals have lost a sense of historic connection between principles and the struggles that brought them into being. In their "ideological boxes" they have distanced themselves from giving a meaningful critique that can be heard by others.[26] Meanwhile the consumerist ethos has extended to ideas where they are seen as so many options to be tried on for size, played with, discarded, without commitment.[27]

The disillusion of a distinctly liberal tradition as a part of the ending of the modern age should be sending warning signals to Unitarian Universalists. Thus far we seem to be backing into the twenty-first century. Some are beginning to take up with the new participatory, "hieroglyphic," mythic cultural orientation, particularly in worship. Others seem resistant or even inertial maintaining a "liberal," verbal, rational, demythologized orientation.

Unitarianism is the child of the same Enlightenment tradition that gave us liberal democracy in the American and French revolutions. It derives from the same dual concern for power and freedom, a generous society and a guarantor of individual human rights, the very liberal tradition defined by José Ortega y Gasset. The same impulse and in large measure the same network which gave leadership to the American Revolution founded Unitarian religion. John Lukacs traces the dissolving of twentieth century populism from a progressive movement to a nationalist orientation. Nationalism he says is the enemy of liberalism. Liberal populism has given way to a nationalist socialism. He sees nationalism as the "myth of the people" more basic than a state, so powerful that for masses of people it becomes a substitute for religion. From the late nineteenth century nationalism has turned anti-liberal with negative attitudes towards "aliens" in its midst, for example anti Semitism. Hitler exploited the emergence of national socialism, an underlying force that survived him.[28] Lee Harris sees the discrediting of liberalism with its inability to actually see the non-rational forces underlying the catastrophe of World War I and therefore its inability to prevent World War II and subsequent threats to civilization.[29] Duncan Howlett sees a collapse of religious liberalism in the 1920s in Europe and the 1930s in America. In parallel a discredited liberalism involved an inability to see its own contradictions, in Protestant Christianity an inability to be thoroughgoing, true to itself.[30] Lee Harris calls the extreme form of this, a fantasy ideology, an inability to see the messy processes of what is but to wish instead what ought to be full grown from the head of Zeus. The abstract trumps the actual, rendering would-be liberal critiques detached and unheeded.[31] We can see this kind of "liberal" reacting well advanced in Unitarian Universalist congregations today.

If such an emerging picture captures something of the epochal transition we are experiencing, how will our three models of congregational life fare in the near future? The first, an organic picture as in Puritan times, has largely been forgotten, morphed into a collective global networked electronic polity.[32] The second natural rights or individualist model is in danger of becoming an artifact[33] as it becomes increasingly difficult for mature autonomy of thought in a participatory fragmented and noisy environment. The key here will be the ability of some to find solitude for reflection, for cultivation of the conscience, for an original connection of ideas, which they may then bring to the gathered congregation. And the key for our third model will lie in viable sustained commitments in pluralistic congregations, the willingness and ability of groups to challenge each other even as they encourage each other with appreciation and understanding. A blanket acceptance of any and all ideas without critical review, bringing them to clarity, and making choices would only create a post-modern muddle without any strategic vision of a congregation's ministry. A well honed pluralistic congregation is required of us if we are to minister to a pluralistic society, in a painfully divided world.

I have shared with you three historic models for congregational life labeled the organic, the individual, the pluralistic. Each and all are in a trial for survival and for their effectiveness in a rapidly changing society we must engage, confront, leaven and even lead.[34] Strong inertias and affirmations can be seen acting in congregational life from all three models, whether from the first model, or the two which depend wholly upon voluntary participation in a free association. We turn now in the next two lectures to philosophies which inform us and a characteristic in our history which may bring to focus a vision for ministry going forward.

Those who believed no truth could exist unless encased by the burrs of opinion went away utterly baffled. Sometimes they thought he was on their side, then presently would come something on the other. He really seemed to believe there were two sides to every subject, and even to intimate higher ground from which each might be seen to have an infinite number of sides or bearings, an impertinence not to be endured! The partisan heard but once and returned no more.

—Margaret Fuller[1] (on Emerson)

CHAPTER THREE

Transcendentalism and Its Transformations

THOSE WHO BECAME KNOWN AS TRANSCENDENTALISTS began gathering in the fourth decade of the nineteenth century. The movement pretty much dissolved two decades later. What is remarkable is that the legacy of this movement remains at the center of Unitarian and Unitarian Universalist discourse to the present day. Here we will attempt to identify what ideas brought them together, what they may have accomplished, the transformations of key ideas as Transcendentalism dissolved and how in the present day Transcendentalist influences make creative partners in theories of key importance to liberal forms of religion today. Transcendentalism is the subject of a large field of scholarship. I shall be sparing and selective as we try to understand the significance of the brief flowering of what we call New England Transcendentalism.

The movement developed with the coming together of a dozen or so Unitarians and their friends, and dissolved in the next generation or half-generation of Unitarians and their friends into a diverse number of projects and orientations. Somehow this brief and sparse group has inspired us ever since.

When we think of the Transcendentalists the town of Concord first comes to mind. However, Boston, as we stressed in chapter two, was the head of the New England body and the center of Massachusetts ecclesiastical life. And Concord, in an age when people walked places, was a day's walk from Boston. Several thousand British colonial troops remembered this vividly! Boston became the location of the American Unitarian Association in 1825, seven years before Ralph Waldo Emerson resigned his ministry of the Second

Church. Other Transcendentalists who served Boston pulpits were George Ripley (13th Congregational), Cyrus Bartol (West), Theodore Parker (West Roxbury and 28th Congregational), William Henry Channing (Religious Union of Associationists), Orestes Brownson (Society for Christian Union and Progress), Samuel Johnson (Christ Church, Dorchester), Samuel Longfellow (28th Congregational), William Roundsville Alger (New North and Bulfinch Street churches and Mt. Pleasant Congregational Society), John T. Sargent (Suffolk Street Chapel), and James Freeman Clarke (Church of the Disciples) who was influenced by Transcendentalism but bridged with the more "conservative" Unitarians.

In addition Bronson Alcott conducted his Temple School in Boston, Elizabeth Peabody owned her famous West Street Book Store and organized America's first kindergarten there, Margaret Fuller's "Conversations" for women were held in Boston, Brook Farm was in West Roxbury, a town later annexed into the City of Boston, and the Transcendental Club held a majority of its meetings in Boston. Octavius Brooks Frothingham, radical preacher in Salem and New York, retired back to Boston to write and was founding president of the Free Religious Association which held all but one of its annual meetings in Boston.

The chief opposition to the Transcendentalists came from Boston and Cambridge. The great polarity between "conservative" Unitarians and the Transcendentalists served to coalesce the movement and to put it on the map. The other polarity was the Concord-Boston tension. Sometimes, like Mohammed moving out of Mecca to Medina, it is important to leave, to intensify your position(s) and perhaps eventually to prevail. So it was for Alcott, Margaret Fuller for awhile, Ellery Channing the nephew, Elizabeth Hoar and Henry David Thoreau (natives of Concord), and most of all the central figure in the movement, Ralph Waldo Emerson.

The foremost criticism of the Transcendentalists today is that they could not form their own institutions, indeed were anti-institutional. In 1836 a small group gathered soon to be known as the Transcendental Club. It was loosely formed and dispersed in four years when there was not enough agreement to hold it together. Key members were Frederic Henry Hedge, its convener, Ralph Waldo Emerson, George Ripley, Orestes Brownson, Theodore Parker, Margaret Fuller, Elizabeth Hoar, and its elder diplomat, Convers Francis. The glue, if we can see new ideas as a cohesive force, was German Idealism, especially that of Immanuel Kant, and the English romantics, particularly Coleridge and later Carlyle, together with their opposition to Lockean empiricism which at that time informed the Unitarian mainstream. It would seem there was enough there to keep an informal group of intellectuals organized for more than four years.

Before I look at several of these key players there are two qualifications on the oft leveled criticism that Transcendentalism was anti-institutional. It is true that the Transcendental Club, *the Dial*, their journal, and Brook Farm proved to be quite transient but in all fairness, there was no lack of institutions around them. Creating institutions was not a priority for the times. It was the inertia and creative dullness of existing institutions which called them out, particularly the resistance of the Divinity School to new ideas, only 17 years into its existence.

Secondly, the Transcendentalists created a new form of institution seldom acknowledged, namely, the individual. Called out as individuals, engaged in original and creative work, producing literature, ideas, solutions with which large numbers in society resonate, the individual, whether intentionally or not, becomes an institution. Emerson is the archetype for this form but it became an American phenomenon: Edward Everett, for example, Unitarian minister turned public orator; Walt Whitman, the poet; Robert G. Ingersoll, the great free thinker; or that latter-day Transcendentalist of the twentieth century, R. Buckminster Fuller, to mention a few. There was a certain impatience among the Transcendentalists to re-form, to get on with their work, to reflect upon their vocation and create something unique, to break into history with a fresh revelation, pure, sky-borne, electric. The institutions of religion, even free, liberal, and democratic, at best tolerated them as mavericks. Schools of Divinity and the fellowshipping processes tend to weed out what Emerson called the poet-prophets.

Let's sketch briefly the careers of several of the inner circle Transcendentalists. It should become clear that the centripetal forces came to predominate with one exception, Ralph Waldo Emerson himself, who held the center, indeed who was the center.

George Ripley graduated from the Divinity School and was immediately ordained as minister of the Thirteenth Congregational Church in Boston in 1826. After a gestation period of ten years he burst onto the public stage in a dispute with that pillar of Unitarian orthodoxy, Andrews Norton. The "miracles controversy" broke out in 1834 when Ripley preached a sermon identifying the ideas of Jesus as true not because Jesus spoke them but that he spoke ideas of universal validity. Directly in opposition were the Lockean inspired "conservative" Unitarians who saw miracles as tangible proof of the authority of Jesus, ergo his ideas are true. George Ripley was responsible for translating key works of German Idealism into English. In the tradition of Idealism universal ideas are inborn and only need to be recognized, nurtured and expressed. Authority resides within, readily accessible through our intuition, and is trustworthy. His sermon anticipated Theodore Parker's South Boston sermon by seven years.

Towards the end of his tenure at Thirteenth Congregational both Ripley and a minority in his congregation grew restless. They felt he was too "liberal" and he felt the pew proprietorship system killed voluntary initiative among members. In 1841 he resigned to found together with his wife, Sophia, and several others the experiment in collective living at Brook Farm. The seven year run of Brook Farm was notable, if brief. Founded on the principle of equality and the exercise of choice in engaging one's share of the work that will lead to the success of the whole, the experiment early on focused on farming and educating both day and residential students. Had they stayed with this formula Brook Farm might have succeeded but in what some felt was reckless speculation other occupations were added, an ambitious but under-funded building program was undertaken, and with the rising agitation in society for workingmen's rights the core members including Ripley transformed their focus to the Fourier socialist model of community, expiring in 1847. George Ripley then went to New York and a career in journalism.

The founder of the Transcendental Club was Frederick Henry Hedge who graduated from the Divinity School in 1828, two years after Ripley, and took up the ministry of what is now the Arlington Center church. The first Unitarian to serve there, Hedge after about two years was embroiled in a split in the Parish between the Unitarians and the Universalists. After several seasaw congregational meetings the controversy was resolved and the Universalists withdrew to form their own society. But the remnant was weak and Hedge's salary was in arrears. The loyalists were used to his long sermons laden with a heavy Hegelianism. As soon as things quieted down Hedge felt he could resign and he journeyed to Bangor, Maine, where the Independent Congregational Society was more than capable of paying his salary and enjoyed his improving sermons for fifteen years.[2]

Hedge was strongly influenced by the Hegelian form of German idealism. For Hegel Spirit articulates itself through nature in time to a world or absolute idea. History is an organic process, whereby the primitive (embedded in nature) is opposed by the emergent forces while at last the synthesis of the two by holding both (Hegel calls it "negativity") re-forms the process into a new whole; that whole is sponsored by a people coalesced into their nation-state. The first step is subjective, opposed then by an objective reaction, then brought together in an absolute. Thus the poetry of the individual is opposed by the prose of the opposing critical responses, brought into a whole by a collective narrative regulated by a people in their state. There is assumed to be a great release of freedom in this synthesis, collected from a narrative Hegel calls World-History.[3] While for Hegel the nation state pulls history along, for Hedge it is the church. Somehow a Catholic matrix is countered by the Protestant principle, critically dispersing in numerous sects. For Hedge Unitarianism in its openness and non sectarian broadness can be the instrument for coalescing the church together forming a new synthesis, pure Christianity, pure Spirit. We must avoid the temptation to build a separate sect but instead by example leaven all sects to a catholic embrace. This is Hedge's vision of the Hegelian Absolute Spirit, the workings of that rational unity unfolding as World-History.[4]

Hedge's vision is not wholly incompatible with that of Theodore Parker, for example, in that both saw an absolute, but for Parker it is a unity behind diversity whereas for Hedge it was a unity as the culmination of diversity, what he called the broad church. While all the Transcendentalists share in common their view that reason, the underlying reality of idealism, is superior to the understanding, which can only extend as far as the senses can sense and the understanding can integrate, never the less the heavy handed monism of Hedge's Hegelianism, as we shall see was poles apart from Emerson's ideal of the individual as poet-prophet. Indeed a powerful ally of Emerson's in post-colonial India, Rabindranath Tagore, protested Hegelianism as oppressive and imperial, excluding not only emerging non European peoples, but the individual poet singing of the realities of nature and everyday original experience. Culmination it seems comes not at the climax of history as in Hegel but in the unique and original act of creation, the work of the poet of life.[5] In Emerson's words (in *Self-Reliance*):

> Society never advances. It recedes as fast on one side as it
> gains on the other. It undergoes continual changes; it is
> barbarous, it is civilized, it is christianized, it is rich,
> it is scientific; but this change is not amelioration. For
> everything that is given something is taken. Society
> acquires new arts and loses old instincts.[6]

Hedge then in his "broad church" orientation with time became quite acceptable to the mainstream of Unitarianism. His resistance to sectarianism found a ready response among Unitarians who still felt at home in the organic model of social responsibility for the wellbeing of all as it had been in the days of the Standing Order. No such reception awaited his colleague Theodore Parker.

A third member of the Transcendental Club, Parker was a complete alternative to the ecclesiastical orientation of F. H. Hedge. Parker began as the young minister out in West Roxbury in 1837, becoming easily the most audacious of the core players, burning his way through life and through Boston like a bright comet. He was the least subtle, advocating his Absolute Religion widely and thoroughly. Like Ripley he advocated the universality of basic religious ideas, implanted in human nature as a Divine presence, spoken by the great teachers and prophets of humanity, including Jesus. It was a universal Theism with a positive view—in Parker's words—of "the adequacy of man for all his functions."[7] Religious authority resided in the intuitive grasp of Divine truth within, the higher reason that is the primary revelation, scriptures being secondary but confirmatory. Scriptures may give empirical confirmations to the understanding reinforcing reason which provides truth to the intuitive mind. In Parker we see a concern to reinforce personal intuitive insights with the human cultural record and he learned a dozen languages to do so!

He is even better known for his advocacy of reform issues, particularly the abolition of slavery. His schedule, both scholarly and prophetic, was so extensive he died before his fiftieth birthday in 1859. In his last 14 years he was minister of Boston's largest church, the Twenty-eighth Congregational Society, numbering 7,000 members with weekly attendance in the great Music Hall numbering in the thousands. It is likely his membership exceeded the sum total of congregations of all the mainstream Unitarian ministers who refused to exchange pulpits with him!

Margaret Fuller was the smartest of the inner circle, passionate, seeker of truth, gadfly. Her adult life may be divided into three chapters until her untimely death at age 40: (1) as a central figure in Transcendental circles, (2) her journalism career, and (3) life in the Italian Revolution of the late 1840s. Before teaching French and German in Bronson Alcott's Temple School in Boston, Fuller had been well known among Divinity students in Cambridge as a frank and challenging intellect which they dare not ignore. Her standing was further enhanced by several series of "Conversations" for women she led in Boston on literary and philosophical issues, each session composed of 25 paying participants. Perry Miller paints a picture of these forays:

> Margaret Fuller presided over these bacchantic rites in homemade dresses that her adorers thought to be of Oriental magnificence, and at the climax of each session, when she had reduced the others to awed silence, she would close her eyes in an inspired trance and utter, unfathomable words, which they thought emanated from some occult or Delphic wisdom.[8]

She was of course a member of the Transcendental Club and in 1840 became the first editor of *the Dial*, easily the leading literary and philosophical journal in America. It was here her fame as America's first literary critic became established as well as her work translating and interpreting Goethe. In this period she declined to join Brook Farm. Not only was she independent but a certain restlessness pervaded her life. By 1843 she traveled west with James Freeman Clarke and on her return transformed her diaries into the book, *Summer on the Lakes*, describing the Great Lakes, the vanishing of the native peoples and transforming of the landscape by the new settlers. Among her observations for example was the omni presence of pianos, obsolete for frontier life, always out of tune, enough to spoil the ear of any would-be musician.[9]

Wider perspectives characterized her work later as literary critic and first woman reporter for Horace Greeley's New York Tribune. Her great surviving work, central in the women's suffrage movement, was *Woman in the Nineteenth Century*. The last decade of her life mirrors a classic tragedy. Visiting Europe as a foreign correspondent, in the midst of her interviews she became attracted to the Italian Revolution, in Rome fell in love with a young nobleman, one of its leaders and fought with them against the French siege of Rome which they lost. She, her nobleman, Ossoli, and their son, booked passage for America and perished at sea in a storm within sight of land. For our purposes, however, her great role was to push issues with the leaders of Transcendentalism, so that they better grasped and articulated the significance of the American Romantic movement.

The fiery Orestes Brownson started out a Universalist, left the ministry, inspired by Channing reentered as a Unitarian serving the Society for Christian Union and Progress in Boston for seven years, gradually grew impatient with the liberal movement and its wealthy merchants and strongly agitated for the inclusion of the working classes. Disillusioned, he joined the Roman Catholic tradition, editing *the Pilot* and advocating rather reactionary values in society.

Bronson Alcott, a self-educated philosopher and genius with young children, founded three educational experiments, the most famous, Temple School in Boston. For his pains to treat children with respect as equals, and in Boston for admitting a black girl as student, his schools all collapsed. Like Fuller he was famous for his animated "Conversations" but unlike her he was a disastrous writer and depended on others, particularly his friend and neighbor in Concord, Emerson, to prepare his works for publication. His educational theories, based on Pestalozzi, had more success in old England than in New England.

Henry David Thoreau once said he had the largest library in Concord and all the same title![10] We cannot discuss Transcendentalism without mention of Thoreau. But it is wise to remember that the books we read and admire such as *Walden* or *A Week on the Concord and Merrimack Rivers*, were not popular in their time. But for Thoreau to be original, to be true, to intensify privacy in order to see the mists of prejudice through which we view the world, rising in the early morning light when they can be observed, this was more central than book sales. He could earn pin money in the pencil factory. Thoreau felt he could travel the world living in Concord. He read and absorbed the scriptures of India and China into his experience, lived them as a "sojourner in civilization." In 1838 he polled out of the Town (Unitarian) Church as he would pay no taxes to support his father's minister. August found him on the Concord River, immersed in nature, mythology, childhood memories:

> The sound of the Sabbath bell, whose farthest waves are at
> this instant breaking on these cliffs, does not awaken
> pleasing associations alone. Its muse is wonderfully
> condescending and philanthropic. One involuntarily leans
> on his staff to humor the unusually meditative mood. It is
> as the sound of many catechisms and religious books
> twanging a canting peal round the world, and seems to
> issue from some Egyptian temple, and echo along the shore
> of the Nile, right opposite to Pharaoh's palace and Moses in
> the bulrushes, startling a multitude of storks and alligators
> basking in the sun. Not so these larks and pewees of

Musketaquid. One is sick at heart of this pagoda worship.
It is like the beating of gongs in a Hindoo subterranean
temple.[11]

He found he could support his life with six weeks' work a year, he built
his own house (on Emerson's property) for a two year experiment. Its greatest
benefit was perspective.

Our village life would stagnate if it were not for unexplored
forests and meadows which surround it. We need the tonic
of wildness...[12]

While his mentor, Emerson, saw Life as a power floating all animate
beings, and Hedge found Hegel's Spirit unfolding in history, Fuller saw
Truth, Ripley a socialist vision, Parker an Absolute beneath all transience, for
Thoreau that force was directly apprehended Nature, wild Nature. And then
of course it works both ways for he also observed:

What is Nature unless there is an eventful human life
passing within her? Many joys and many sorrows are the
lights and shadows in which she shows most beautiful.[13]

The Transcendentalist movement was a brief episode lasting 30 years at
best, a generation and a half. In 1832 Ralph Waldo Emerson resigned from
Second Church and in 1835 moved to Concord. 1834 saw Bronson Alcott
founding his Temple School in Boston. In 1836 Ripley and Norton engaged
the miracles controversy, Emerson published "Nature," and Hedge convened
the Transcendental Club. In 1838 Emerson preached his Divinity School
Address and Orestes Brownson began publishing the radical Quarterly
Review. In 1840 Margaret Fuller inaugurated her "Conversations," the Dial
began its meteoric four year history, and Brook Farm organized. In 1841
Parker preached his South Boston sermon, "The Transient and Permanent in
Christianity," leading in 1845 to his call to the Twenty-Eighth
Congregational Society. In 1841 as well Emerson published his First Series of
Essays. In 1843 Fuller serialed what later became her great feminist tract, in
1844 Emerson's Second Series was published, in 1846 Thoreau set up his
Walden experiment to be written up for publication in 1854. In 1844
Brownson converted to Catholicism, in 1850 Margaret Fuller died, in 1860
Theodore Parker sailed for Florence to die there, in 1862 Thoreau died.
Emerson lived another 20 years but his best work was completed. In other

words Transcendentalism can be telescoped between two major events, the disestablishment of religion in Massachusetts, 1833, to the outbreak of the American Civil War in 1861.

After the Civil War in this vast land somehow a new order of life took on more reality than Transcendental idealism. The merchants of Boston were now industrialists and their wives increasingly Episcopalians. Minot Savage at the Church of the Unity was preaching Charles Darwin and Newton and Priestley. The American philosophy of choice was becoming Pragmatism. The Free Religious Association, organized in 1867, contained two parallel strands, one being the gathered remnants of Transcendentalism, among them the aged Emerson, and the other being the scientific Theists led by Savage and Francis E. Abbot. Transcendentalism had entered American culture as a kind of folk philosophy headlined by Emerson's essays and poems. And Thoreau's *Walden* also became a classic for American literature.

To generalize, at the opening of the fourth decade of the nineteenth century Unitarians in Boston were the leaders of American intellectual culture. Into this pond dropped the Transcendental movement, America's version of European romanticism and idealism, making itself felt in ever widening circles in literature, philosophy and reform. We have sketched the contributions of all its core members except one: Ripley, Hedge, Parker, Fuller, Brownson, Alcott, Thoreau. From the start and as long as he lived, Ralph Waldo Emerson held the center and I would contend has been a core influence to this day among Unitarian Universalists. His views seem to be a kind of standard against which or for which ideas are compared.

I cannot hope to discuss his philosophy in any detail here but any bookstore will yield ample scholarship, most remarkably Robert Richardson's recent biography and of course Emerson's own *Essays*. Instead I will use his key ideas as points of connection with five contemporary theories I consider of critical importance for our ministers and congregations today. By points of connection I do not imply a cause and effect relationship, only that a bridge can be readily made between the Emersonian standard and these important contemporary theories.

Emerson's *Divinity School Address* of 1838 is one of our classics known to just about every Unitarian Universalist. Much has been written about it, particularly as it relates to reforming, or enlivening the ministry and conduct of worship. It was another early presentation of an idealist rather than a Lockean empiricist view. And as Conrad Wright has pointed out, Emerson was still in a vocational crisis six years after resigning from Second Church.[14]

He had left in order to save his soul or to be a better minister in himself. He had left it to practice it. But the reaction to his *Address* slammed the door to any lingering thoughts of return.

Why was the reaction so completely negative among mainstream Unitarians of the time? It seems to me what was not in the sermon was as incendiary as what was there. There was not one Biblical quote, text, reference or exegesis. He mentions Jesus in a special way along with Zoroaster, Moses, Zeno, St. Paul, George Fox, Swedenborg, Washington, the Wesleys and Oberlins, the Hebrews, the Hindus, and the gods, Osiris and Apollo. He defers to Palestine, Egypt, Persia, India and China. But not one direct Biblical reference. His only quote was a line from Wordsworth:

A pagan, suckled in a creed outworn...[15]

only adding insult to injury, at least to an Andrews Norton who had made a living and reputation in Biblical exegesis and teaching it to the likes of Emerson. He was preaching after all in the Divinity School chapel! As a young man about to prepare to enter the school, Emerson had asked Channing for a reading list. Back had come a list of *Bible* commentaries. This had not been what he was seeking from the great founder. Now Emerson was not only breaking theologically from mainstream Unitarianism, he was leaving the authority of revealed scriptures altogether to join philosophy. He was leaving Jerusalem and Christianity and taking up Athens and Philosophia.

The term, "Philosophia," was invented by Wilfred Cantwell Smith of Harvard to explain a unique quality in the western branch of human culture. Unlike any other branch, in the West we "have" religions. In all others religion is embedded, even when there may be several traditions present. Can it be then that what is called "the West" is a religion? The classical western tradition, which he identifies as rationalist-idealist-humanist, is a religion in that it affects lives, people live by it and it is a religious faith. The West "has" Christianity, Judaism, Islam, and these have profoundly interrelated and mutually influenced each other, but there is—i.e. we live within—Philosophia.[16] In this context I am reporting that Emerson simply left Christianity and took up with Philosophia.

Huston Smith supports Wilfred Smith in identifying Philosophia as a great world religion and adds important qualifying definitions.[17] This identification so dramatically illustrated in our Emersonian tradition is important for at least two reasons. (1) What we might call the Transcendental conversion in Unitarianism did not happen in Universalism until living memory. The Universalist mainstream was Biblically based well into the twentieth century and for the most part was simply forgotten as the Unitarian-type influences came in. (2) Philosophia could provide an important way by which different elements of Unitarian Universalism can articulate their commonalities and their differences. Emperor Justinian did, after all, close the pagan Academy in Athens in 529 A.D. and here it is, much enriched and elaborated, fifteen hundred years later.

Another of Emerson's core contributions was his vision of history, an alternative to the "onward and upward forever" view of "progress" that has been so persistent. With quiet humor he once used the term "up and onward" and again at another time, "onward and onward," but as we saw in the discussion of Hegel he opposes "progress" with a biographical assessment (in his essays *History* and *Self Reliance*):

> All history becomes subjective; in other words there is
> properly no history, only biography.[18]

> No greater men are now than ever were. A singular equality
> may be observed between the great men of the first and of
> the last ages; nor can all the science, art, religion, and
> philosophy of the nineteenth century avail to educate
> greater men than Plutarch's heroes, three or four and
> twenty centuries ago. Not in time is the race progressive.[19]

This brings us to Emerson's individualism. It is clear what history should be about is the creation of individuated and virtuous individuals. He addressed himself to the individual with the challenge to pull ourselves up through the press of society around us, to leaven the context as we go, but with the moral obligation to develop ourselves as the centerpiece of life. This is not selfish, or self-centered, or solipsistic as is often levied. In the present time it is said to be anti-community or to deny our interdependence. I think Emerson would reply that unless people develop in themselves as moral and spiritual persons of integrity, entering into community would be a hollowness or a dependency, not a true interdependence.[20]

When Rabbi Edwin Friedman developed his theory of leadership in congregational systems (as in family systems) his central point was that leadership can only be effective through self-differentiation, as opposed to the herd mentality or togetherness. When the leader is not self-differentiated the anxiety level in an organization accelerates, the weak and dependent rule, and any initiatives by individuals are sabotaged.[21] Historically we might say that had Emerson not left the movement in a sense, had he not been highly differentiated in his *Divinity School Address*, Unitarianism would probably not have followed him, might even have become a fossil religion like Swedenborgianism or the Shakers. Or to put the issue another way, perhaps the Transcendentalists and mainstream Unitarians of the time needed each other, were two sides of the same coin of emerging Unitarianism.

Another theory that must be wrestled with if we are serious about the individual among us and about spiritual development as many of our congregations claim to be, is the present day work of Robert Kegan at Harvard on the adult orders of consciousness. There is not space here to develop his definitions so I commend his book, *In Over Our Heads*, for your attention.[22] The challenge for a congregation is a spiritual discipline, to support those in one order of consciousness while simultaneously encouraging the next order at a more complex level. In addition is the phenomenon of still another order of greater complexity, those like Emerson who tend to migrate out of congregations into larger informal connections.

We have used the terms soul and self several times. For Emerson soul is the Divine spark within, the power which sustains us, the source of authority, the source of conscience or the moral sentiment connecting us to the moral order, the guide for personal virtue. The oversoul is the awareness that the same power within which energizes us is the power in all which energizes the world. From soul comes what he calls reason whereby through the intuitive function we gain access to Truth, as opposed to sensation which in the Lockean system develops only to the point of understanding. In his essay, *Compensation*, Emerson writes:

> There is a deeper fact in the soul than compensation, to
> wit, its own nature. The soul is not a compensation, but a
> life. The soul is. Under all this running sea of circumstance,
> whose waters ebb and flow with perfect balance, lies the
> aboriginal abyss of real Being. Essence, or God, is not a
> relation or a part, but the whole. Being is the vast
> affirmative, excluding negation, self-balanced, and
> swallowing up all relations, parts and times within itself.[23]

And in *Spiritual Laws* and *Oversoul*:

Place yourself in the middle of the stream of power and wisdom which animates all whom it floats and you are without effort impelled to truth, to right, to a perfect contentment.[24]

When it breathes through his intellect, it is genius; when it breathes through his will, it is virtue; when it flows through his affection, it is love.[25]

I included enough here to indicate what I believe is a problem for us in Emerson. His soul is a bit too pat, too perfect, even rosy. The details of his life are far more various and real.[26] Here I see the psychology of Carl Jung to be a critical corrective in our time. Van Wyck Brooks sees Emerson's over-soul as an equivalent of Jung's "collective psyche" (or more accurately, collective unconscious).[27] In actuality Jung's concept is more multifarious than Emerson's and the balancing of the eruptions of the collective unconscious in the wholeness of self is a process Emerson would have acknowledged I think from his own experience. (And I must add for those who have studied Jung's personality typology, much of what Emerson identifies as reliance upon "intuition," particularly when he speaks of "conscience," is actually introverted feeling which in Emerson's own consciousness is matched with extraverted intuition, INFP.[28])

We turn lastly to Emerson's relationship to Nature. Before Darwin published his *Origin of Species* Emerson was reflecting upon the unfolding processes of nature which he called metamorphosis. Above the beauty of the underlying integrity, nature is always in flux, always changing forms. Emerson hopes and strives for more insight, as he reveals in *Nature*:

There is in the woods and waters a certain enticement and flattery, together with a failure to yield a present satisfaction. This disappointment is felt in every landscape …It is an odd jealousy, but the poet finds himself not near enough to his object. The pine tree, the river, the bank of flowers before him does not seem to be nature. Nature is still elsewhere…The present object shall give you this sense of stillness that follows a pageant which has just gone by. What splendid distance, what recesses of ineffable pomp and loveliness in the sunset! But who can go where they are, or lay his hand or plant his foot thereon? Off they fall from the round world forever and ever.[29]

He is not expressing an alienation here, rather an entrancement, a search never ending, a longing unrequited. Here is the Transcendentalist romantic probe, that beyond every circle of experience, every circle of capturing the idea or principle there, you are seeing, indeed, another circle opening.

If Emerson can be regarded as the great American individual of the nineteenth century, standing as a solitary institution in his own right, in the following century using the same image we must focus upon R. Buckminster Fuller. Here was the inventor of the geodesic dome, and of the dymaxion house and dymaxion map, the world game, the holder of dozens of patents for his inventions, the author of numerous books of poetry and prose on philosophy, education, design science, mathematics and geometry, one of which, *Synergetics*, could someday be a candidate for inclusion among the world's scriptures.[30] Fuller self identified as a latter day Transcendentalist. After-all he was the grandnephew of Margaret Fuller and grandson of a minister of the New North Church in Boston. He was one of "the fighting Fullers" which inspired a professor listening to him to write a poem in 1969:

> Fuller is a name
>   For better or for worse,
> Of two who grappled
>   With the universe.
> "I'll accept it,"
>   Said the famous spinster.
> "I'll explain it,"
>   Said the bold Buckminster[31]

Just as a moment of great crisis in Emerson's life was the act of opening his first wife's tomb to stare at its contents, Fuller climbed a bridge in Chicago and meditated on the edge whether or not it was better to jump or to live. He chose life. And immediately went into a two year vow of silence, emerging resolved to be original, to take nothing second-hand, to have "no more secondhand God."[32] Likewise, Emerson wrote a poem after the tomb experience and his resigning from the ministry of Second Church:

> I will not live out of me
> I will not see with others' eyes
> My good is good, my evil ill
> I would be free.[33]

For both individuals the imperative to be original was central and formative for the remainder of their lives. As Fuller's biographer, Applewhite, put it:

> Somewhere in the course of this transcendent spiritual crisis
> it is certain that Fuller visited a past or future landscape of
> astronomically remote philosophic distance. It has always
> been my suspicion that some part of him remains in that
> alien country of his self-discovery, that he has never fully
> returned.[34]

That perhaps is the message the Transcendentalists have for us through all their transformations, that life to be lived rightly and fully, must be original. It is the most critical and difficult spiritual learning of our lives. You leave one setting and you arrive at another for the same reason, to listen to the universe within yourself, to give what you know in your mind and heart to the world, to enter into life fully. "To thine own self be true." This daemon of Socrates, of poet-prophets everywhere, of Emerson and of Fuller is the vocation of the minister of religion whether in Galilean hills, in apricot groves of Chu Fu, beneath the Bo Tree, in church or lyceum of New England.

CENTER: First Church In Boston, 1630; with sister Unitarian churches, the oldest in New England.
CLOCKWISE FROM TOP LEFT: First Church in Plymouth, 1620; First Church in Salem, 1629; First
Parish in Watertown, 1630; First Church in Dorchester, 1630.

Charles Chauncy

Jonathan Mayhew

Theodore Parker

William Ellery Channing

Three Ages of Ralph Waldo Emerson—as a young
man, at mid-life and as an elder.

Ken Patton

A Temple of Humanity, the Charles Street Meeting House in Boston featured a claiming of our global inheritance from the many branches of human religious culture. Shown here is one of the author's favorite items in the congregation's extensive art collection, a Yoruba statuette from Nigeria. Kenneth Patton was minister of the congregation which gathered in a circle for its worship.

O poet!…Thou shalt have the whole land for thy park and manor, the sea for thy bath and navigation, without tax and without envy; the woods and the rivers thou shalt own, and thou shalt possess that wherein others are only tenants and boarders. Thou true landlord! sea lord! air lord! Wherever snow falls or water flows or birds fly, wherever day and night meet in twilight, wherever the blue heaven is hung by clouds or sown with stars, wherever are forms with transparent boundaries, wherever are outlets into celestial space, wherever is danger, and awe, and love,—there is Beauty, plenteous as rain, shed for thee, and though thou shouldst walk the world over, thou shalt not be able to find a condition inopportune or ignoble.

—Ralph Waldo Emerson[1]
The Poet

CHAPTER FOUR

From Unsectarian Sect to Multifaith Faith

IN PREVIOUS CHAPTERS, WE EXPLORED our grounding in the New England matrix, looked at three models for how we have structured congregational life and we considered our philosophical development in Transcendentalism and particularly western 'Philosophia.' Here we will take our polity and tradition and relate these to how we might focus our ministry for the world around us going forward. What are the particular realities calling us to ministry and what in our experience makes us increasingly prepared to carry forward this ministry? What does the world require of us? To this question I respond, we are called to be multifaith congregations with an interfaith ministry.

Living in the spaces between and among groups and individuals descends appropriately from our first model of congregational life (and even from Hedge's "broad church" ideology). That is where the established ministers in Massachusetts were instituted to live. Hence even long after disestablishment in 1833, Harvard President Kirkland's assessment of Unitarians as the "unsectarian sect" held true. Likewise the individual responsibility for spiritual development, encouraged in the context of congregational life, enlists the special power of our second model. And pluralism must be a given for a multi faith congregation. In addition a grounding in Emerson's philosophy with the kinship of five contemporary orientations provides an axis and powerful orienting resources. (These five were Philosophia and the theories of Friedman, Kegan, Jung and Buckminster Fuller.) Identification of Philosophia in the West for example unlocks one of the three major complexes of global religion (the others being India and China). Keeping in mind then these structural and philosophical considerations we turn first to what degree we may be prepared to enter into interfaith ministry.

Unitarian encounters with the branches of world religion are clustered in three phases, the first being quite miscellaneous. Early Unitarianism was embedded in Christianity and the Enlightenment. Interest in non Christian traditions was by way of general interest reading with some effort at comparing and contrasting from their own Christian base. Joseph Priestley, English Unitarian who immigrated to Pennsylvania in 1794, wrote an exploratory work called, "*A Comparison of the Institutions of Moses with those of the Hindoos and Other Ancient Nations* ... published in 1799. He lays the groundwork for his and our interest:

> Every thing of great antiquity relating to any part of the
> human species must be interesting, not only to their
> posterity, but to all mankind; as the institutions of their
> remote ancestors must be capable of receiving some
> illustration from the knowledge of them.[2]

Herrlee Creel gives a persuasive analysis of the influence of Confucian traditions on the French Enlightenment. Indeed he asserts that "literate Occidentals knew more about China in the eighteenth century than they do in the twentieth." He quotes Reichwein in a discussion of Voltaire: "...Confucius became the patron saint of eighteenth-century Enlightenment."[3] It is safe to assume of many of the older clergy of Boston and environs, as O. B. Frothingham mentions of his father, Nathaniel, minister of the First Church, that they had translations of oriental scriptures in their libraries. William Bentley, early Unitarian and minister of the East Church in Salem, learned to read Arabic, and through the ship captains in his congregation became an Asian expert and founder of Salem's East India Marine Society. In the early Republic relations with Arabic speaking countries were often mediated through his translations and advice.

The second phase, or what I call the Theistic phase, of the Unitarian relationship with the whole of human religion began with the advent of Transcendentalism. Even a cursory reading of Thoreau's *Walden* introduces the reader to Chinese and Indian literatures. He singles out the *Bhagavad-Gita* as a source of his daily reading before the morning trip to his well. *Mencius* is compatible with his view of resistance to absorption into the social herd. His friend, Emerson, makes fewer references in his published *Essays*, perhaps because they were delivered in lyceums to general audiences, but it is clear he is deeply literate in Chinese, Indian, Persian and Arab sources. His poem, *Brahma*, penetrated beyond the vast apparatus of the Hindu pantheon to its deeper orientation, much as in the second chapter of the *Bhagavad-*

Gita. His quotation from *Mencius* in the essay *Experience*, shows a genuine sympathy with Confucian understandings of nature and humanity's shared space. But the most profound global orientation for Emerson is captured in his essay *The Poet*, where he announces the world significance of every original poet-prophet. The poet represents our humanity. The poet-prophet breaks into history much as an avatar would, an incarnation, sky to earth, long awaited, bringing beauty, truth, good. The poet-prophet announces life, the wholeness of life in the "enchantments of nature." The poet is a great emancipator, announcing change unceasing, metamorphosis. Emerson's *The Poet* could well serve as a text for a world centered ministry!

The later Transcendentalists refined, elaborated, fleshed out an emerging orientation to world religion but never exceeded Emerson's transforming *The Poet*. Theodore Parker proposed his "Absolute Religion," that inspired source of truth behind all forms and teachers of it, but in a way froze this into a Theistic boundary. His methodology involved following up an intuitive grasp with an empirical documentation in the "Sacred Books" of humankind. He listed six traditions in which he worked extensively: Christianity, Judaism, Hinduism, Buddhism, Classic (or what Smith called Philosophia), and Islam.

The second generation of Transcendentalists and others of the Free Religious Association completed what Emerson, Thoreau, Parker began, and brought to a head what we can characterize as the second, or Theistic, phase of Unitarian attention to our world religious inheritance. In 1874 well-known Unitarian hymn writer, Samuel Longfellow in an essay, *The Unity and Universality of the Religious Ideas*, identifies the branches of world religion as "churches of the One Living God" and as "the birthright Church of man."[4] His vision was more lofty than his word choices. But his hymn is often sung to this day, *Light of Ages and of Nations*. Another great hymn of this group by William Channing Gannett, *It Sounds Along the Ages*, is perhaps the closest to an ethnic Unitarian hymn with the phrase, "the oracles of Concord one holy word declare." Samuel Johnson, the other hymn writer of the famous "Sams," wrote the hymn, *Life of Ages*, which like Longfellow's and Gannett's assumed a Universal God, working through "the prophet's word and the people's liberty."

> Never was to chosen race
> that unstinted tide confined;
> yours is every time and place,
> fountain sweet of heart and mind.[5]

Johnson wrote a three volume work, *India, China,* and *Persia,* a massive life-work, and perhaps the first comparative religious study which treated each religious tradition as an equal and on its own terms in its own context. In his introduction to *India,* in 1873, he wrote:

> It is only from this standpoint of the Universal in Religion
> that they can be treated with an appreciation worthy of our
> freedom, science, and humanity. The corner-stones of
> worship, as of work, are no longer to be laid in what is
> special, local, exclusive, or anomalous; but in that which is
> essentially human, and therefore unmistakably divine. The
> revelation of God, in other words, can be given in nothing
> else than the natural constitution and culture of man. To be
> thoroughly convinced of this will of itself forbid our
> imposing religious partialism on the facts presented by the
> history of the soul.[6]

Both "Sams" briefly served congregations in Boston and went on to distinguished ministries elsewhere, Longfellow to Germantown, PA, and Johnson to the Free Church in Lynn. Perhaps the most popular essay and often reprinted as a pamphlet by the Free Religious Association was by Thomas Wentworth Higginson and called *The Sympathy of Religions,* published between 1855 and 1898 in English and French. This was a popular way of summarizing what he characterized as "under many forms...but one religion, whose essential creed is the Fatherhood of God and the Brotherhood of Man."[7] Some substituted symphony for sympathy. The pamphlet is heavy with classical Western and Hindu references (particularly of the Brahmo Samaj) with only passing mention of the Buddha, Mohammed, Confucius, and Zoroaster. He did develop his special interest in Buddhism elsewhere.

The Theistic phase developed in the networks around the Free Religious Association (FRA) and climaxed with Chicago's Parliament of World Religions in 1893. Midway through his FRA presidency in 1872, Octavius Brooks Frothingham gave a lecture on the philosopher Comte. This indicates that while the idea of a synthetic Universal Religion, as it was often called, was in the air in Europe, India and America, it was focused by the Free Religious Association. Frothingham in addition was reaching beyond the Theistic consensus with Comte, for example these lines from his lecture:

> Every religion is entitled to be called a religion of humanity,

because every religion aims at the good of humanity.... Every religion is entitled to be called a religion of humanity as being a product of humanity.[8]

In 1872 also, William J. Potter, Unitarian minister in New Bedford, gave his secretary's report to the FRA anticipating the World Parliament by 20 years:

> Some of us may live to see the day when there will be a
> world convention...of representatives from all the great
> religions of the globe, coming together in a spirit of mutual
> respect, confidence, and unity for common conference on
> what may be for the best good of all; not to make a
> common creed by patching articles together from their
> respective faiths in which they might find themselves in
> agreement, but, emancipated from bondage to creed and
> sect, to join hands in a common effort to help mankind to
> higher truth and nobler living. It may be that the work of
> this Association will culminate in such a world's
> convention, a peace convention of the religions.[9]

Twenty years later this is exactly what happened and Jenkin Loyd Jones, the prime mover of the World Parliament, told the FRA they were the ground breakers that made it possible.[10] In 1893 Potter announced (a bit prematurely we can say) that humankind was "in the birth-struggles of a new religion."[11]

In isolated places it began to look that way, in Samuel Johnson's Free Church in Lynn, in Moncure Conway's South Place Chapel in London and Frothingham's Independent Liberal Church in New York. A parishioner describes the manner of opening worship in Frothingham's church:

> The preacher rises, and receives close attention. The book
> which he usually reads is one compiled from the sacred
> scriptures of many ancient nations, and entitled "The
> Sacred Anthology;" a work arranged by Moncure D.
> Conway..."Listen," he says, "to the teachings of the ancient
> scriptures. This is from the Hindu;" or, "This is from the
> Chinese;"...thus giving no precedence in authority to any
> selection, but valuing each for its beauty, wisdom, piety,
> and internal truth.[12]

Moncure Conway was considered one of the Transcendentalist circle, but spent most of his career in England. When at Harvard Divinity in 1853 he journeyed out to Concord and took a walk with Thoreau. When Thoreau asked him what he was studying he replied, "The Scriptures." Thoreau then asked him, "Which Scriptures?" Thoreau had once confessed that he knew the scriptures of the Hindus, Chinese and Persians better than those of Judaism.[13]

An important publishing event in the 1870s and 1880s was James Freeman Clarke's two volume, *Ten Great Religions*, which was reprinted through 19 editions. It was successful while the far better work by Samuel Johnson was a dismal market failure. In contradistinction to the FRA circle, Emerson and Thoreau, Clarke's work was Christocentric, believing that a global religion would emerge from a broadened form of Christianity. Beginning right at the flyleaf of volume one, Clarke presented a diagram of the importance of each of the ten religions. Judaism was at the center of the circle, surrounded by four quadrants labeled "Christianity." Arranged outside the circle were his remaining eight religions: Greece, Buddhism, Brahmanism, Zoroaster, Scandinavia, China, Egypt, and Islam.[14] His major distinction is between "ethnic and catholic religions." Of the three catholic religions, Islam, Judaism and Christianity, he sees the latter as forming the "future religion of mankind." Not even Buddhism is considered "catholic." He presents an evolutionary view, with demons and dreams the most primitive, followed by polytheism and idolatry, then pantheism and finally of course the emergence of monotheism, and of these the supreme form, given the life of Jesus, Christian Theism. He does not seem to realize, as his more sophisticated contemporaries in the FRA do not either, that half the world's religious traditions since the axial age have been oriented around naturalism and humanism. But we can summarize that in the second and Theistic phase of Unitarian relating to the branches of world religion, Clarke's perspective held a much wider response in the general public than the scientific, absolute or universal theism of others we have discussed.

At the turn of the century, and through World War One, the broad engaged vision of a coming together of religions faded. With the waning of the Free Religious Association a certain impatience with the pace of adaptation and the reactivity of Unitarianism continued. It was a time of New Thought movements, the Theosophical Society and various Spiritualist impulses, energized largely in diffuse networks, notably in Greenacre, a summer retreat center in Maine, 1894-1916, for example. Leigh Schmidt called the tendency an "increasing liquidity of liberal religious identities."[15]

Adrift from the relational disciplines of congregational life, and connected in largely transient networks, gains of the second phase went into abeyance.

Much of the energy flowed to the "experts" in universities with the rise of departments of comparative religion, and the study of religious culture as sociology, anthropology or even archeology. George Willis Cooke for example wrote *The Social Evolution of Religion* (introduced by the young John Haynes Holmes) in which he discussed the history of religion in terms of the organization of society in each stage, with extensive sociological descriptions without advocacy except for a vague optimism.[16] Earlier one of Unitarianism's most popular preachers, Minot Savage, who published dozens of books some in many editions, up to and past the turn of the century, did not discuss the world's religious traditions except to point out that if all scriptures are considered to be revealed by their respective adherents, they could not all be right and thus all are reduced to very fallible status along with all sectarian interpretations of them. Even as late as 1936, Louis Cornish gave a report for the Commission on Appraisal on the "International Relations" of the American Unitarian Association, focused on Christian "liberals" and Unitarians in America, Europe, the Philippines and India, plus the Brahmo Samaj. He summarized the umbrella of inclusion: "All share the same vision of man uplifted from sordidness and sin into the embodiment of the Divine."[17]

In short there was a gap in vision and attentiveness to our world religious inheritance for several decades at the opening of the twentieth century, well past the first World War and of general attention even to the end of the Second. There were a few exceptions, the development of the International Association for Religious Freedom, from mostly a liberal Christian focus with some liberal Jewish and Hindu participation to the full multi religious body it is today; the work of William James on *Varieties of Religious Experience*, narrowly focused but the beginning of a phenomenology of religion, and of course the work of psychologist Carl Jung with universal religious symbolism and motifs of mythology, archetypes of the collective unconscious, differentiation of the psyche and individuation of consciousness. Scholarship in the history of religion and comparative religion has tended to develop at some distance from public and congregational attention, narrowly specialized and relatively inaccessible.

Phase three, or the humanistic phase of the Unitarian attention to our world religious inheritance, arose slowly from within the emergence of religious humanism. Typical of early humanist writings is the little book by

Curtis Reese, called *Humanist Religion*. Reese advocates taking the scriptures of the world down from their pedestals of revealed authority and adding to them a more extensive religious literature. Reese edited a collection called *Humanist Sermons* in 1927 which included "The Humanist Religious Ideal," a sermon by A. Eustace Haydon, professor of comparative religion at the University of Chicago. His summary right at the start is a bit more exuberant than most of his generation:

> In these days of the religious sciences, if one is to interpret
> religions at all he must do it in terms of our human,
> planetary quest. To gather the history of religions of the
> planet into a single sentence, one must say that it has been
> all, all the long labor of it, the effort of human groups to
> wring from their environing, natural world a satisfying life.
> It has been the unconquerable thrust of the spirit of man
> for realization, for the good and complete life.[18]

We can say however that this is a vision of the purpose of religion, bringing out from academia a concern for a world orientation. Haydon was one of 34 ministers and professors to sign the Humanist Manifesto in 1933 composed of 15 affirmations much in line with Haydon's vision. Thus it was in 1933 that the American Unitarian Association perceived it was time to ask one of the leading humanist ministers to write a pamphlet. John Dietrich was chosen and wrote:

> The civilized world is rapidly being reduced, by common
> means and methods, to a community; and naturalistic
> Humanism, I believe, will be the life-philosophy of that
> world community.[19]

Perhaps the most enlightened of the early humanist attempts to organize an appropriate religious congregation was the collaboration of Clarence Skinner (Universalist) with John Haynes Holmes (Unitarian) and John Herman Randall (signer of the Humanist Manifesto) in the formation of the Community Church in Boston in 1920 on a nonsectarian basis. I included this congregation in *The Boston Religion* as it eventually affiliated with the Unitarian Universalist Association in 1968. This is one of the few experiments where humanism was organized on a mass basis, often filling Symphony Hall where it met each Sunday, 1927-1942. While it is described in detail in *The Boston Religion* it is appropriate to cite the first line of its membership covenant which summarizes its perspective:

> The Community Church is a free fellowship of men and
> women united for the study and practice of universal
> religion, seeking to apply ethical ideals to individual life
> and the co-operative principle to all forms of social and
> economic life.[20]

A large number of Unitarians and Universalists later took this generic vision
in 1961 as a basis for what has become known as "Unitarian Universalism."

Kenneth Patton began his ministry in Boston at the newly organized
Charles Street Meeting House in 1949 on a similar basis.[21] In his *A Religion
for One World* he cited A. Eustace Hayden's "quest for a good life" as the basis
for religion everywhere in every time. For example (in *Man's Search for the
Good Life*):

> ...on the social level, religions were a sign that the world
> was unsatisfying—not good but to be made good. They
> were the continuation in a more complex social form of the
> struggle of organisms to secure from the natural world the
> values which make life good.[22]

Though the Charles Street Meeting House experiment lasted only a
quarter century I consider it the most important institution to be formed by
Universalists and Unitarians in the twentieth century. It was a temple of
human religion marshalling the art, poetry and music of our world religious
inheritance for liberal religious worship. Its controversial presence was not
primarily in its humanism and naturalism but in its innovations in the forms
of worship and architecture opposing deep inertias in liberal religious practice
Patton called "orthodoxies of form." As with most orthodoxies those inside
them hardly perceive the hard shells of protection arrayed around them.
Innovation is perceived as attack. Thus a temple of and for one world,
bringing into one worship space our human inheritance, creating new
expressions of worship, including a loose leaf hymnal rendering weekly
printed orders of worship obsolete, resulted in wide unease, particularly as the
sale of materials exceeded the ability of the meeting house to turn them out
of its 'do it yourself' printing press. (All of this developed, of course, before
the advent of the computer with desk top and web publishing and even copy
machines.) In retrospect it is not really surprising that the bureaucracy at
"headquarters" failed to implement the idea of subsidizing a UUA

"Department of the Religious Arts" at the Meeting House even after it was endorsed by the Commission on Art and Religion. Orthodoxies protect their own.

In Patton we see the tradition of the poet-prophet identified by Emerson come to renewed attention among us. In *A Religion for One World* it was given a chapter:

> When we cease ascribing the religious scriptures to the revelation of the gods, to whom then do we give credit for the bibles of humanity? There is only one possible answer: we must thank the poets of the human race. Religion is [our] impassioned affirmation of life....Our religion is our love affair with life, and no [one] who is not in love with life has a religion worthy of the name. Our religious scriptures, the basic ones and the most used and most influential of all the religious writings, are love poetry. They are love songs written to project our love of life, of humanity, of nature, of beauty, of wisdom, of goodness into expressions of power and celebration. A work of art is an act of celebrating a portion of reality. The art of religion is the most composite and consummate of all the arts, the art of life itself.[23]

In the introduction to his remarkable anthology, *The Chinese Poets of Nature and Humanity*, Patton identifies for his world poet four candidates. "Naturalistic and realistic religion has four great poetic prophets: Walt Whitman, Pablo Neruda, Chuangtzu, and Tu Fu."[24] In his last major anthology, *The Way for This Journey*, he includes 10 as a portion of his "Bible of Humanity:" Lao Tzu, Chuang Tzu, Confucius, Mencius, Tsze Sze, Hsun Tzu, Buddha, Hui Neng, Huang Po and Nietzsche.[25] He further describes in *A Religion for One World* his concept.

> The prophet-poet is the person who is able to ingest the experience and aspirations of his people. He embodies the most profound assumptions and hopes of his people....Thus he is representative of them all. He is not an elected representative, as are the members of the House and Senate, but by his own abilities, his fitness of identification and comprehension, he creates a valid forum within his

own mind and emotions, wherein the debates of his people
can take place. If in the churning processes of his
integrative and creative imagination he can find answers to
the dilemmas of his time, he becomes a new prophet.[26]

He cites the announcement of Jesus: "I come that you might have life, and
have it more abundantly."

A major part of Patton's work was the combing of our global inheritance
for the forms and meanings, in art and literature, which could enrich our
religious life. His searches took him to the world's oldest surviving tribal
traditions of the K'ung bushmen of Southwest Africa, compiling a book of
stories and songs, *Kaggen The Mantis*. In the preface he records:

The Bushmen had no gods, relating in their myths to the
sun, the stars, the wind. Many of the animals had once
been "people of an early race," who later assumed their
animal forms and behavior. Kaggen was one of the early
race, who became the insect, the praying mantis.[27]

One of the most beautiful poems included was called "The Broken String:"

There were people who
Broke the string for me.
Therefore the place has become strange
to me on account of this.
Because of the string that was broken for me,
Therefore the place does not seem to be,
On account of this.
For the place feels as if it were empty before me.
Therefore the place feels strange to me.[28]

We need to ask at this point if there is a continuity between the history
we have sketched thus far and the history after merger of the Unitarians and
Universalists in 1961. It seems to me, after some early aspiring to fulfill what
had been rather strikingly begun in phase three just discussed, that the string
has to a large extent been "broken." Or to paraphrase the haunting expression
in *Exodus*: "There arose in Egypt a Pharaoh who had not known Joseph."

Merger began well enough with worship in Boston's Symphony Hall and
a stirring sermon by Don Harrington on "the unitary character of the human
family" and "the universality of truth." One of his examples:

> Many thousands have married across faith lines and are
> looking for a common ground of belief. They have fallen
> between the exclusive faiths and are looking for an inclusive
> faith by which to live in dignity and freedom—for the
> welfare of all…We can be that faith![29]

The phenomenon of interfaith families, many with children, has only increased in the intervening 45 years since 1961. Yet there is little notice of them in UUA literature and there are no UUA curriculum offerings addressing the special issues of interfaith households. Congregations with a few or many interfaith members seldom mention let alone develop special patterns of attending to or sponsoring their particular presence. So far even those leading efforts to grow the religion have given no special attention to this unique opportunity for ministry.

Two years later in 1963 UUA commissions reported their assessments and strategies for the future in *The Free Church in a Changing World*. The report of Commission VI, "World Religion and Outreach" was oriented as if there had been no history in the interim since the demise of the FRA and its network of authors. It began with a corporate definition of religion oriented towards "The Divine." There are constant references to "other religions" or "other world faiths" (Other than what?) while priority was given to relationships with "our own religious tradition, the Judaeo-Christian heritage." The Commission set up a 'straw' model, the "desirability of one world faith" or "a universal religion" and then proceeded to caution against "essentialism" or sectarian assumptions that narrow awareness of the variety of religious experiences, an "over-harmonization" or a "syncretism." There was an unidentified quote acknowledging an alternative model practiced in the Association but no development of this model illustrated dramatically by the Charles Street Meeting House, at that time at its peak of effectiveness. The phrase quoted was "not one world faith but a religion for one world." This was an obvious reference to Patton's distinction between a synthetic model of a universal religion and his model as a religion capable of embracing the world of human religion, "a religion for one world." The recommendations of the Commission were based on its preferred dialogue model encouraging talking with representatives of religious groups at retreat centers, listening to music, foreign study, for example. This arms-length approach to world religion indicates the preponderance of academics on the Commission, some not affiliated with the U.U.A. There was little about transforming congregational life as had been proposed in the example of the

Charles Street Meeting House. One would have to conclude there was a studied avoidance of taking note of any of the innovations existing there at the time, indeed a betrayal by this Commission and the administration of the UUA itself.[30]

A UUA pamphlet *Unitarian Universalist Views of World Religions* published a decade later included a section by a member of Commission VI, Harry Hoehler, listing four alternative approaches: (1) hostility, (2) assuming one's own religion is the fulfillment of all others, (3) the synthetic approach for a universal religion, and (4) "the way of dialogue" learning from "other" perspectives, but deepening your own loyalties. Fortunately the pamphlet also included a section by Kenneth Patton which was none of the four. Discussed at greater length in *The Boston Religion* this section ends with Patton's warning:

> I find the whole construct of "World Religions" distasteful
> and historically questionable. Can we not rather ask how
> the religious liberal relates to the religion of humanity?[31]

The UUA's most recent edition of this pamphlet has removed both Hoehler's and Patton's contributions.

In 1967 the UUA issued its *Report of the Committee on Goals* which of course suffers from the drawbacks of all data collection, as opposed to construction of experiments, models and tangible philosophies. But one question was noteworthy for our theme. It asked: "Which one of the following best describes where you would prefer the Unitarian Universalist Association to be theologically ten years from now?"[32] The four choices with percentages are:

> Closer to liberal Protestantism 06.4
> Closer to the ecumenical movement within Christianity . . . 04.8
> Closer to an emerging, universal religion 36.7
> Closer to a distinctive, humanistic religion 52.0

In other words all but 11 percent of respondents preferred to focus the resources and creative energies of the UUA and its member congregations in fulfilling the promise of what we have called the third phase of the Unitarian and Unitarian Universalist emergence in a multi faith world. The Goals Report may represent the statistical high tide of this vision. Certainly the Association's resources have not been focused in this direction despite constant evidence of a wide affirmation of this vision for its religious future.

To give an example, in 1984 at the General Assembly in Columbus, OH, when the Purposes and Principles statement for the UUA Bylaws was proposed, there was no reference to our world religious inheritance. Donald Harrington, Homer Jack and others were attempting to rewrite the "Jewish and Christian teachings" phrase to make it more inclusive. I believed they were dissolving the integrity of that statement while adding little support for a broader global affirmation. Instead I proposed an additional phrase "Wisdom from the world's religions which inspires us in our ethical and spiritual life." Opposed by the Planning Committee I resubmitted it on the floor of the Assembly, and after successfully defeating an unfriendly amendment which would have inserted the word "other" before the word "world," it passed with hardly any opposition.[33]

I believe there are several inertial realities still operative in Unitarian Universalist practice which perpetuate the reluctance to face into a world-centered vision for the religion. The first, of course, is vocabulary and word choice, something the women's movement discovered early. Word choice determines habits of thought. The word "other" mentioned above, "other world religions," requires the prior question, "other than what?," if it is to be used. To answer this prior question can reveal hidden assumptions perhaps not even intended. Another term used by many of us, "world religions," needs reexamination as Patton pointed out above, for historical reasons. The term "denomination" too implies that Unitarian Universalism is a part of something larger, usually Christianity. This is a rather arrogant assumption. The word "church" presents its own problem, at minimum for would be participants who have Judaism or Islam as their religion(s) of origin. An examination of vocabulary is essential in providing an opening for interfaith ministry.[34]

The religious arts are critical influences more powerful than the spoken word. Examples abound when music or stained glass windows are incongruent with themes important for a congregation living within their influence. Indeed the structure of inflexible pews in a rectangular room facing a raised altar and pulpit is a minority form deriving from ancient mystery religions in the middle east where the miracle was performed by a secretly initiated priesthood behind the railing at the altar. It is a non-democratic and non-universal form, unlike the circle or flexibility in worship forms. More often than not the context, particularly if it is beautiful music or architecture, overwhelms words or contrary aspirations or visions of the people.

A third inertia of the system is the education of ministers, which still reflects intentionally or unintentionally the world view and functions of the Christian priesthood. Many of our heroes are those who overthrew, at least in part, what they were educated for (or worse, trained for) in theological schools. At a time when so many ministers are burdened with educational debts, an evaluation of education for Unitarian Universalist ministers is long overdue.

A goal for a multifaith faith must be the formation of global consciousness, an orientation in which the world holds our first loyalty, in which world citizenship comes first and the practice of religion holds our human inheritance as our birthright. A religion for one world lives in the reality of that NASA image of a blue and white sphere as our home, what Buckminster Fuller called, "Spaceship Earth." That reality and that inheritance is evolved through the fires of the individual's own spiritual development, always unique and always responsive to the requirements of the human family, its every day, its world themes and challenges. In other words through the cultivation of global consciousness in each individual Unitarian Universalist, congregations become more capable of ministering to the world which desperately needs global perspectives.

An example of this need is before us on nearly every evening's newscast. Samuel Huntington in his book *The Clash of Civilizations* has put forward the idea that there are nine world civilizations, with fault lines keeping them apart: Western, Latin American, African, Islamic, Sinic, Hindu, Orthodox, Buddhist and Japanese.[35] This theory is yet another "East is east and west is west and never the twain shall meet." Huntington counters the whole drama of human emergence on the planet and six thousand years of history recording the interdependence and mutuality of influence among the branches of human culture. In addition I have identified in the book *Growing Your Spirituality* what I call the "spiritual origins archetype" or Archetype of the Spirit which informed the world before the advent of literacy and can be seen in religious motifs on all inhabited continents to this day.[36] The *Archetype of the Spirit* can be recognized world around today, consciously or unconsciously in religious responses.

There is evidence that the majority in the general public today are only able to perceive the world in a flat earth perspective, my nation or ethnicity first, as a fortress surrounded by alien or even hostile strangers. But just as the ideology of Malthus supported the ambitions of the East India Company in late eighteenth century, the ideology of Huntington in the post-cold war reinforces the neoconservatives of advanced capitalism in their efforts to divide and conquer world markets. In this context the idea of dialogue as an end point of interfaith relationships only reinforces such ideologies. Honing the qualities and stages of development in the individual of a full global consciousness is the primary task of congregational life in our age. Corporately nurturing the formation of planetary individuals and the projecting of global perspectives in society is our first priority.

The formation of a global consciousness for a multifaith world will depend not only upon taking up with the world's scriptures and spiritual literature, but will require a thoughtful implementation of theories of human development such as were discussed by Robert Kegan,[37] and a grasp of the variety of religious experience and response within our world inheritance such as I developed in *Four Spiritualities*.[38] Henry Rosemont gives as an example a Confucian developmental theory, leading to the shengren.

> As we follow that path, we will be led to see ourselves less as free, autonomous, unchanging selves/souls, less as altogether distinct from the physical world, and more as co-members of a multiplicity of communities, who, through sustained effort, are increasingly integrated into an ever-larger community, something larger than ourselves. We must come to see and feel ourselves as fundamentally, not accidentally, intergenerationally bound to our ancestors, contemporaries, and descendants. It is not that we are to become selfless, i.e. altruistic, for this would imply an isolated self to be surrendered, the pure existence of which any Confucian must deny; rather must we come to see and feel our personhood as dependent on others for its uniqueness, just as others must depend on us for their uniqueness: in order to be a friend, or a lover, I must *have* a friend or lover; and "freedom" must be seen not as a state of being, but as an achievement for each of us.[39]

This goal in a Confucian context can be seen as compatible with Kegan's fifth order of consciousness, what I would identify as a full global consciousness. Placed in world history it can be seen as the uncoiling of suchana, "the incipience of sheer possibility" as Guha points out,[40] or the "tacit dimension" which Polanyi develops, that "creative releases are controlled, and yet never fully determined, by their potentialities."[41] In our time of increasing fearfulness and conservativism, perhaps a pervasive loss of nerve, when many are driven away from reflective thought, a provincial view of the world can be quite demoralizing. A wider perspective of increasing global consciousness can be a source of hope.

Fifty years ago, Muhammad Asad, in his *The Road to Mecca*, described his journey from his origins in Europe to his conversion to Islam. He served as Pakistan's first ambassador to the United Nations, knew intimately most leaders of the Middle East and lyrically describes his experiences of desert religion. Having in mind the picture of earth photographed from the moon, in a personal reach of global consciousness, I read this passage of Asad's describing his walk seven times around the Kaaba in the hajj.

> I walked on and on, the minutes passed, all that had been small and bitter in my heart began to leave my heart, I became part of a circular stream—oh, was this the meaning of what we are doing: to become aware that one is a part of a movement in an orbit? Was this, perhaps, all confusion's end? And the minutes dissolved, and time itself stood still, and this was the center of the universe....[42]

Afterword

THERE IS ONE RESOURCE UNITARIAN UNIVERSALISTS have, unlike any possessed by even the most enlightened global networks (electronic or friendship based) or think tanks or diplomatic negotiators or arms-length interfaith "dialoguers" cannot have: autonomous congregations. As we have seen there are more than two and a half centuries of broadening perspectives, experienced, mediated and tested in congregational life. It is one thing to travel the globe or to absorb and integrate an increasing global consciousness as an individual sojourner. It is quite another to ground it in the reciprocity of shared and ongoing congregational living and commitment. To be present, to listen and to speak, to be generous and exacting, these are the fires in which ministry and mission are formed, tested, readied for the world.

The congregation is a unique contribution of Protestant Christian traditions in the West. It takes religious community beyond the compact villages of kinship and tribal traditionalism found still in most of the world. It moves beyond the sangha or refuge of Buddhism or the concern to intensify and inculcate traditions of the synagogue. Congregations embody the gospel to be preached to the world. To form and find commitment to a mission in the world implies a human emergence on the planet into the light. Honed for centuries, husbanded/nurtured, it is time to bring an expanded mission from our Unitarian experience into a global embrace.

Congregational life with an expanded mission will not be easy. And it never has been benign. It is the most exacting spiritual discipline on the planet, requiring knowledge, vision and patience. Knowledge must include not only our world religious inheritance but also a grasp of how our human nature unfolds developmentally in the individual from cradle to grave and how congregational systems may be supportive of all, evolving in their capacity to serve a global society. A vision must appraise opportunities for a congregation's ministry grounded in continuity with its Unitarian and Universalist past, accurate in its assessment of resources and experience available to it, and challenging to push its frontiers further with embracing globally focused ideals. Patience is seldom found alongside knowledge and vision. After all impatience with the pace of change in orthodoxies energized Unitarian and Universalist founders from the beginning. But change in ourselves and others, and in voluntary and democratic bodies, is a patient process.

Individuals come into our congregations from many backgrounds. As we noted in chapter one it takes time to grasp the complexities inherent in the story of our emergence among religious alternatives, to truly understand what we are and the common threads of our theological history requires time and reflection. Newcomers always enter our midst in a story or even pilgrimage rich and unique. Their religious past and their experience in that past always brings to us insights and new influences for the congregational whole. Assimilation is a two way street of listening and responding, building a new participation.

Of particular importance are interfaith families who enter a congregation with different individual journeys already underway in parallel. (This is true for all but usually high profile in interfaith families.). Each adult, each child, has their own past and their own unfolding. A congregation must be generous, attending to each journey opening before each individual. Resources must be suggested outside the congregation's home environment as well as within it (Catholic retreat centers, Jewish or Hindu festival celebrations, Buddhist meditation circles, etc.). Generosity involves as well a process of reporting back, leavening the common congregational experience. The concept of conversion from "other" to "us" is obsolete, even destructive, for spiritual growth. It cannot be a condition of membership when a congregation is intentional in its global affirmations.

Congregational cultures and environments vary widely among us. I have served a variety: Midwest Universalist, West Texas frontier, historic New England Unitarian, and suburban informal. Should a congregation inhabit an historic landmark or anchor a central historic function in its city obviously its commitments will emanate from that place and that context. But its ministry will know no bounds short of a world embrace. If a congregation occupies a temple of great beauty, but with messages from a parochial base, it must know that architecture or sculpture and painting or music are far more powerful than the spoken word. Its ministry will always be nuanced by the presence of this beauty. Fighting one's inheritance and environment, living in unhappy incongruence, will only render one's mission ineffectual.

Here I believe Emerson's theological orientation is helpful as a thread running through the varieties of congregational culture. The wisdom to be gleaned in the perspective of philosophia and a view of history not implying "progress" can weave a wide diversity of approaches into a Unitarian Universalist tapestry. Examination of the nature of the self and the differentiation of the individual (Emerson with Jung, Channing, Kegan and Friedman) gives a primary purpose to congregational life. This is sharpened and embraced by the presence of nature: its wildness (Thoreau), its metamorphosis or evolution (Emerson, Darwin), the necessity to understand it (R.B. Fuller), to ensure the human posterity within it (i.e. the prophet-poet, Emerson or Camus), an entrancement in its mystical reality (Emerson, Patton), its abundance for us, to love life, to worship (Emerson, Tagore, Patton), all of these requiring that life be original, individual. If the Unitarian Universalist movement can find an Emersonian thread it will be able to see its emerging pluralism, not as a compromise but as a means of moving forward into the world which needs its presence. The Unitarian Universalist religious complex may yet become unstuck, finding its purpose in the whole, becoming more capable of ministering to a multifaith world.

The minister in a pluralistic congregation ministering to a pluralistic society has one great focus: she or he brings to the congregation—to the world—perspectives that can hold it and lead it into life and light. Ministers to fulfill their office must be prophet-poets. They minister to congregations, but as in the critical distinction Jesus made in the *Gospel of John*, they are in their congregations, not of them. Ministers will give of their lives to their congregations—to the world—but sooner or later like Lao Tzu (or Emerson or Jesus or Socrates or the Buddha, etc.) they will leave. The prophet-poets hope their perspectives will leaven and endure even after their presence is forgotten in that nature that is beyond. We are, after all, sojourners in consciousness.

Notes

CHAPTER ONE

1. William Ellery Channing, "The Moral Argument Against Calvinism," Works. (Boston: James Munroe, 18460), Vol. I, pp. 225-6.

2. Chapter 1 is not identical with Lecture 1 in the Minns series as the latter was accompanied by 80 slides of Boston churches accompanied by commentary related to the images.

3. Edwin H. Friedman, *Generation to Generation*. (New York: Guilford Press, 1985), p. 229.

4. This special role of King's Chapel is discussed in greater detail in Peter Tufts Richardson, *The Boston Religion*, (Rockland, ME: Red Barn Publishing, 2003), pp. 26-29.

5. Quoted by Forman, Charles C. in Conrad Wright, ed., *A Stream of Light: A Sesquicentennial History of American Unitarianism*, (Boston: Unitarian Universalist Association, 1975), p. 17. See also M. A. DeWolfe Howe, *Boston: The Place and the People*, (New York: MacMillan, 1903), pp. 190-221.

6. The ministers were William Emerson, John T. Kirkland, Peter Thacher and Joseph S. Buckminster. The laity: Theophilus Parson, John Davis, John Lowell, William S. Shaw, Robert Hallowell Gardiner and Obadiah Rich.

7. Clarke, James Freeman, "The Five Points of Calvinism and the Five Points of the New Theology," *Vexed Questions in Theology*, (Boston: George H. Ellis, 1886), pp. 10-16.

8. As can be imagined the architectural legacy of the Unitarians was considerable from the colonial period. Typical colonial meeting houses had the main entrance door on the long side with the pulpit opposite high on the opposite wall. A steeple might be constructed at a gable end. Examples in Boston include: New Brick (1721), Hollis Street (1732), Federal Street (1744), Jamaica Plain (1770) and Brighton (1744). An older style was the impressive Old North Church (1676) which was constructed in the manner of an English country church but in wood. A stone Anglican style church is of course King's Chapel (1749). The most imposing building was the Old Brick Church (1713), similar in appearance to the Old Ship Church in Hingham except it was three stories with two balconies inside with the town clock on the roof.

The Brattle Square Church, located where the Boston City Hall now stands, was an extremely early example of the Federal style built in the late colonial period (1773). A cannonball from Washington's siege of Boston was lodged on its brick façade next to its Palladian window. Other fine examples of Federal style were in Brighton (1809), Dorchester (1816), Roxbury (1804) and the Theodore Parker meeting house in West Roxbury (1773 and later). The Harvard Church in Charlestown (1819) had Bulfinch type features around its windows and doors. Several congregations built Bulfinch buildings: Hollis Street (1787, his first), New North (1804), New South (1814, his masterpiece), Federal Street (1809, his only attempt at Gothic), and when Unitarians financed the building of the first Catholic cathedral Bulfinch, a member of King's Chapel, supplied the design. Another prominent Federal period architect and member of First Church was Asher Benjamin who designed its fourth meeting house (1808) as well as the West Church (1806, his masterpiece). His Charles Street Meeting House (1807) was originally designed for the Third Baptist Church, a far less complex and ornate performance.

The Greek Revival style, aside from the splendid porch of New South's Bulfinch building (1814), included the Hawes Place (1832), Twelfth Congregational (1824), Mt. Pleasant Congregational (1846), Third Religious Society in Dorchester (1840), East Boston (1852), Friend Street Chapel (1828), and the splendidly ornate Church of the Unity (1860). There were no wooden examples of Gothic Revival. However there was a large group of heavy stone Gothic structures, most notably the fifth meeting house of First Church known as the "Westminster Abby of Boston" (1868), the early transition style of Jamaica Plain (1854), the Church of the Saviour/Second Church (1845), East Boston's second building (1867), the Hanover Street building of Second Church (1845), Thirteenth Congregational (1848), Brighton (1895), All Soul's in Roxbury (1888), and West Roxbury (1900). There were only two attempts at Romanesque, both in the Back Bay: H. H. Richardson's Brattle Square building at Clarendon and Commonwealth (1873) and the Hollis Street/South Congregational building at Exeter and Newbury streets (1884).

Several important buildings remain for special notice. The Arlington Street Church (1861) designed by Gilman, Fox and Bryant, was modeled after St. Martin-in-the-Fields in London and the Church of the Annunziata in Genoa. The third meeting house of the Hollis Street Church (1810) was once a landmark in today's theater district with its towering steeple. The South Congregational Church on Union Park Street (1861) was important for sheer size. The Church of the Disciples in the same neighborhood (1869) was rather homely on the outside but remarkable inside for the play of natural light in the worship room, reinforcing the emphasis there of congregational participation. The Channing Church in Dorchester (1900) was a pleasant example of the Shingle style, unlike its cousin on Norfolk Street (1890) which must have garnered an all time prize for ugliness. The last meeting house of Second Church on Beacon Street (1914) was a masterpiece of Neo-Georgian style designed by Ralph Adams Cram. First and Second Church at Berkeley and Marlborough (1972) is a rather successful "phoenix" design rising from the ashes of fire. South Boston produced two ugly buildings, Unity Church (1856) and the Hawes Unitarian Church on Broadway (1872). The Theodore Parker Memorial (1873) at the corner of Berkeley and Appleton streets excelled in both ugliness and impracticability.

In summary, the Unitarian churches of Boston purchased 104 buildings and occupied an additional 51 meeting halls for their worship. A fair percentage of their efforts had redeeming qualities. The moral of this discussion of architecture must be that beauty reinforces all other religious values, particularly when the design is congruent with the integrity of religion practiced there. Unitarians built a number of outstanding but fashionable buildings which may have detracted from the effectiveness of their worship and activities. Wood, brick and stone carry more powerful and permanent messages than transient spoken words. One should be able to stand in the middle of an empty building and absorb silent messages pointing to the vision, themes, essence and impact of the religious community gathered there.

9. The slides with accompanying commentary covered three basic visual representations of the central importance of The Boston Religion: (1) a documentation of Unitarian architecture particularly among the older congregations, (2) the Benevolent Fraternity chapels, (3) buildings in neighborhoods later annexed into the city and (4) selected key leaders: Lathrop, Emerson, Freeman, Channing, Gannett, Pierpont, King, Mayhew, Lowell, Hale, Parker, Savage and Tuckerman.

10. A complete listing of Unitarian societies organized in Boston can be found in *The Boston Religion*, pp. 229-231.

11. In *The Boston Religion* I applied the psychological theory of Robert Kegan on the orders of consciousness to the study of Unitarian history in Boston, pp. 220-222. His theory, developed in *In Over Our Heads: The Mental Demands of Modern Life*, (Cambridge: Harvard University Press, 1994) and other writings, has a continuing importance for Unitarian Universalists. If churches and the movement in general are not to go through cyclic implosions as it appears happened in the last half of the nineteenth century when many Boston Unitarians drifted over into Episcopal churches, it will be important to develop understandings on how to support members in the third as well as in the fourth orders. While few in number it may be that the movement loses some of its fifth order participants as well when its programs become too ideological, simplistic and single track, albeit with gentle and liberal intentions.

12. For a discussion of pew proprietorship issues see *The Boston Religion*, p. 175.

13. *The Boston Religion*, pp. 30-34.

14. Quoted, *The Boston Religion*, p. 33.

15. Ministers in the 1890 Boston Social Register were: Unitarians William Roundsville Alger, Stopford Wentworth Brooke, Christopher R. Eliot, S. A. Eliot, George E. Ellis, Octavius B. Frothingham, Edward E. Hale,

Nathaniel Hall, Edward H. Hall, Samuel Longfellow, Andrew P. Peabody and Robert C. Waterston; Episcopalian Phillips Brooks; and John Morison and Leighton Parks. However all the Unitarians listed except one were elders. Perhaps the same characterization might be suspected for the laity. The death of Godfrey Lowell Cabot in 1962 and of Eliot Richardson in 1999, both life long members of the First Church, symbolically may mark the end of an era.

16. At least 529 ministers have occupied Boston Unitarian pulpits including Puritan ministers from pre Unitarian times but not including most associate and assistant ministers, interim ministers, ministers of religious education, student interns, or guest and supply preachers. Pulpit orators and effective preachers have been too many to name but we cannot ignore Joseph Stevens Buckminister who changed preaching from exegetical text working to more literary excellence; his successor Edward Everett the orator; William Roundville Alger or Theodore Parker who preached to congregations of thousands in rented halls; Edward Everett Hale, Brooke Hereford, James Freeman Clarke, Henry Ware, Thomas Starr King, George Putnam in the nineteenth century or John Haynes Holmes, Dana Greeley, Jack Mendelsohn, John Nichols Booth, Kenneth Patton, Carl Scovel or Kim Harvie in the twentieth.

   Boston ministers have been among the great organizers of ecclesiastical, social, literary, justice and parish activities: Charles Chauncy, Andrew Eliot, James Freeman, William Ellery Channing, Joseph Tuckerman, Ezra Stiles Gannett, Samuel Barrett, Charles Francis Barnard, E. E. Hale, Samuel Atkins Eliot, Charles Fletcher Dole, Charles Wendte, Christopher Rhodes Eliot, Clarence Skinner, Dana Greeley, James Allen, Rhys Williams, and more. Radical leadership has emanated from the Boston Unitarians in James Pierpont and Theodore Parker for abolitionism; Jonathan Mayhew for his early Unitarian preaching; Orestes Brownson and William Henry Channing for the rights of laborers, Minot Savage for his pioneering work on theology and the physical sciences; Herman Bisbee and John Turner Sargent who paid their dues supporting freedom of the pulpit; Abraham Rihbany for his timely advocacy for Middle East peace; Donald Lothrop for his defense of the Bill of Rights; Kenneth Patton for his breakthroughs of vision and his congregational model for our future in "one world."

Not surprisingly there have been leaders in liturgy and the worship arts: Kenneth Patton for his open hymnal and world oriented festivals and his proposed "Department of Worship Arts" toward which the U.U.A. turned a deaf ear; Eugene R. Shippen and his wife, Elizabeth, who created striking pageants for the Christian holidays; Palfrey Perkins and Charles E. Park for their prayers; Charles Francis Barnard for his flower festivals, the first in Boston to bring flowers indoors to grace worship; the two "Sams," Longfellow and Johnson, for their major output of hymns we still sing.

The Boston ministers have produced surprisingly few world class philosophers. Known as "the preacher's paradise" perhaps the ministerial mind was not sufficiently challenged in this climate. However the works of William Ellery Channing were read in many languages. Ralph Waldo Emerson was at the center of Transcendentalism in America. Charles Chauncy earlier emerged as the chief apologist to the Puritans among the Arminians. Theodore Parker was literate in 12 languages but did not live to write his definitive works. The writings of Henry Ware, Orville Dewey, James Freeman Clarke, Minot Savage and Charles Fletcher Dole were extensive but not particularly deep. Mayhew, Howard and Lathrop played key ideological roles in opposing British rule. George Ripley was brilliant briefly in the miracles controversy. Samuel C. Thatcher wrote the first published polemic for Unitarianism but long after the fact in 1814. The Transcendentalists Ripley, Emerson, Parker, Brownson, Alger and Bartol were represented but not in the Boston mainstream. Likewise for ministers in the Free Religious Association later, they were represented and supported but not at the center. Scholars included Edward Cummings, John Graham Brooks and James Crooker in the new discipline of sociology and historians included Jeremy Belknap, Thaddeus M. Harris, George Ellis, Octavius B. Frothingham, Henry W. Foote, Joseph H. Allen, Frederick L. Weis and Alan Seaburg. C. W. Wendte was responsible for gathering the works of Theodore Parker into a memorial edition and for organizing and chronicling the early years of International Association for Religious Freedom. And of course Kenneth Patton established a global perspective for the religion with his *A Religion for One World* and other writings. We might include prominent ethicist, James Luther Adams, who for a time was adjunct minister for social justice at the Arlington Street Church. However,

when you consider that we are covering a period of 250 years, that
Boston has been the location of Association "headquarters," that
Harvard Divinity School is just across the river, you have to wonder
how a religion can run on so little intellectual capital. Unfortunately
the current era seems to be its lowest ebb. Channing, Emerson and for
present requirements, Patton, are criticized by many but, be that as it
may, they are what we have to mentor our paths forward.

17. Quoted, *The Boston Religion*, p. 175.

18. In addition to applying to the interpretation of Unitarian history the
theory of Robert Kegan on human orders of consciousness, important
observations on the exodus from Unitarian to Episcopal churches is
discussed by historians Daniel Howe and Ann Douglas. See *The Boston
Religion*, pp. 219-227.

19. Kenneth L. Patton, *A Religion For One World*, (Boston: Meeting House
Press & Beacon Press, 1964), p. 217.

20. *Mark* 8:36.

21. Unitarians have always been reluctant to speak of believing in the first
person plural, "we believe." This distinction between "we believe" (a
creed) and "I believe" (a credo) is critical for each generation of
newcomers. Currently there is widespread misuse of the "Principles and
Traditions" statement appended to the Bylaws of the Unitarian
Universalist Association in 1984. It has increasingly been referenced as
a pseudo creed, "this is what we believe," framed and mounted on
worship room walls. Indeed one version written for children and
circulated in religious education circles begins with the words, "We
believe...." A recent pamphlet of the U.U.A, *Faith Without A Creed*,
for example, begins with the statement, "Unitarian Universalists are
encouraged to question and explore." Then on the very next page we
read: "However, Unitarian Universalist beliefs are consistent with seven
principles..." which are then listed from the U.U.A. ByLaws. Such an
impulse is far removed from the approach of William Channing
Gannett in "Views Commonly Held Among Us," over one hundred
years ago.

22. In most of Unitarian history each generation has seen one or two
theological perspectives in the ascendancy. For two generations in the

second half of the eighteenth century it was Arminianism with some input from Arians and Socinians. Ebenezer Gay, Jonathan Mayhew, Charles Chauncy and James Freeman were prominent. In the transition from "Liberal Christian" to the classic Unitarian Christian generations it was William Ellery Channing who held the spotlight, though many like Henry Ware Jr. and even James Freeman Clarke were to his right. There then were several decades when Transcendentalism electrified a generation and onward. This was followed by the Free Religious Association which composed the left wing of Unitarianism, others continuing in a mainstream led by Gannett, Clarke, Hereford, Hale, Ames and others. The Free Religious Association contained for the most part those who developed further what Parker started with his "absolute religion" either from a comparative religious perspective or from a scientific perspective of blending in the physical sciences. In the early twentieth century while the mainstream continued to assimilate Transcendentalism (including its transmission of "higher criticism" of the Bible), scientific Theism and reworked forms of "liberal" Christianity, in the wider movement Humanism began its ascendancy in the 1920s and '30s led by Curtis Reese, John Dietrich, Edwin Wilson and others. A Humanist—Theist dialectic lasted a good two generations with the former prevailing except in New England. Beginning at mid century a new vision for the movement as a global affirmation of human religion developed, encouraged by the publication of Kenneth Patton's *A Religion for One World* in 1964 and the finding by the Committee On Goals in 1967 that nearly ninety percent of Unitarian Universalists envisioned "a distinctive humanistic" and "emerging universal religion."

Since merger of Unitarians and Universalists in 1961 a number of theological impulses have been imported from outside the movement, "death of God" theology, feminist theology, liberation theology, process theology and various Buddhist perspectives. Mention should be made of the work of James Luther Adams for a theology of ethics and voluntary association, with an important interpretation of the theology of Paul Tillich. A great majority of new ministers educated in non Unitarian seminaries have brought with them prevailing Protestant Christian tendencies. A focused school of thought has not coalesced at either of the traditionally Unitarian schools nor at nonsectarian Harvard. Historically it seems that more "conservative" and more "liberal" wings have needed each other for perspective. But theological discussions must now be one on one so idiosyncratic are theological positions.

23. Emerson says in "The Poet," "the world seems always waiting for its poet."

> The sign and credentials of the poet are that he announces that which no man foretold. He is the true and only doctor; he knows and tells; he is the only teller of news, for he was present and privy to the appearance which he describes.

> The poet is the person in whom these powers are in balance, the man without impediment, who sees and handles that which others dream of, traverses the whole scale of experience, and is representative of man, in virtue of being the largest power to receive and to impart.

In his work, "Representative Men," Emerson defines the role of the poet-prophet in the ongoing human story:

> I must not forget that we have a special debt to a single class. Life is a scale of degrees. Between rank and rank of our great men are wide intervals. Mankind have in all ages attached themselves to a few persons who either by the quality of that idea they embodied or by the largeness of their reception were entitled to the position of leaders and law-givers. These teach us the qualities of primary nature, —admit us to the constitution of things. We swim, day by day, on a river of delusions and are effectually amused with houses and towns in the air, of which the men about us are dupes. But life is a sincerity. In lucid intervals we say, 'Let there be an entrance opened for me into realities; I have worn the fool's cap too long.' We will know the meaning of our economies and politics. Give us the cipher, and if persons and things are scores of a celestial music, let us read off the strains. We have been cheated of our reason; yet there have been sane men, who enjoyed a rich and related existence. What they know, they know for us. With each new mind, a new secret of nature transpires; nor can the Bible be closed until the last great man is born. These men correct the delirium of the animal spirits, make us considerate and engage us to new

aims and powers.

24. Quoted, *The Boston Religion*, p. 14. Poem attributed to Dr. Benjamin Church:

> And Charles Old Brick,
> Both well and sick
> Will cry for liberty.

25. William Channing Gannett, hymn, "It Sounds Along the Ages," in Unitarian Universalist Association, *Singing the Living Tradition*, (Boston: U.U.A., 1993), No. 187.

26. Some might include alongside Chauncy, James Freeman of King's Chapel, who in evolving to a Socinian orientation himself influenced others along the way. In addition Jonathan Mayhew made a fine partner for Chauncy, expressing boldly in his public pulpit what Chauncy more carefully lobbied for among their colleagues and cautiously released in his publications.

CHAPTER TWO

1. José Ortega y Gasset, *The Revolt of the Masses*, (New York: W. W. Norton, 1932), p. 76.

2. The First Parish In Plymouth, Order of Worship, Summer 1975.

3. Alice Blair Wesley, *Our Covenant: the 2000-01 Minns Lectures*, (Chicago: Meadville Lombard Press, 2002).

4. A common vision of Puritan society based upon Isaiah II and Revelation.

5. Reference here is to a family systems concept made popular by Edwin Friedman, for example in his, *Generation to Generation: Family Process In Church and Synagogue.* (New York: Guilford Press, 1985), p. 229.

6. Dependence here is on the author's memory of his memorial service held in the Episcopal Cathedral in Washington, D.C.. Comment was likely on NBC.

7. Ann Douglas, *The Feminization of American Culture*, (New York: Avon Books, 1977), p. 29.

8. Odell Shepard (ed.), *The Heart of Thoreau's Journals*, (New York: Dover,

1961), pp. 6-7.

9. Brooke Herford, *Co-Operative Work In Our Boston Churches*, (Boston: George H. Ellis, 1885), p. 4.

10. Leonard and Mark Silk, *The American Establishment*, (New York: Avon Books, 1977), p. 13.

11. While Mayhew died in 1766 his successor, Simeon Howard, not only continued to preach Mayhew's views in the West Church, he married his widow as well.

12. John Locke, *A Letter Concerning Toleration*, (New York: Prometheus Books, 1990), p. 65.

13. *Singing The Living Tradition*, No. 592. This responsive reading is close to the wording of the original. See Works, Vol. 4.

14. William Ellery Channing, "Spiritual Freedom," Election Sermon of 1830, in *Works*. (Boston: James Munroe, 1843), Vol. III, p. 74.

15. William Ellery Channing, "Remarks On Associations," (Boston: James Munroe, 1843), Vol. I.

16. Richardson, *The Boston Religion*, p. 91.

17. Jack Mendelsohn, *Channing The Reluctant Radical*, (Boston: Little, Brown & Co., 1971), pp. 272-273.

18. Richardson, op. Cit., pp. 93-94.

19. Such a role for a minister as a religious authority counters an emerging model in some quarters of the minister as CEO of the congregation. In a pluralist congregation the minister would need to be familiar on some level with at least the major branches of our religious inheritance and be able to interpret from a global base contextual orientations for a congregation. A model of ministry here would be closer to Rabbi than to CEO. It is important that a minister have the time and take the time for a reading/study cycle in the world's religious scriptures and subsequent writings, to be fluent in chapter and verse and able to interpret and apply such familiarity in congregational life. A cursory course long ago in the so-called world's religions is hardly sufficient.

    Self governing, collaborative lay led religious communities are in an important, often prophetic, tension with corporate culture with its habits of thought and process. A CEO model is particularly inappropriate in a pluralist religion where over half its congregations contain fewer than 100 members. Are not ministers called to a vocation closer to Rabbi than to CEO? Our congregations are filled with competent CEOs seeking out a "minister."

20. Edwin Friedman, *Generation to Generation: Family Process In Church and Synagogue*, (New York: Guilford Press, 1985), pp. 220-249; and his *A Failure of Nerve: Leadership in the Age of the Quick Fix*, (Bethesda: Edwin Friedman Estate/Trust, 1999), pp. 297-306.

21. It seems to me our "unity in essentials" lies in a capacity to bring wider perspectives to matters of theology and spirituality. Unique in emphasis among religious traditions is our motivation to place in the context of a global orientation all more narrowly focused energies. The drama of a global spiritual emergence of our humanity to this point in time, the embrace of one humanity around all local cultural/religious variations, a confidence in the capacities of human nature to live successfully and to survive in collaboration with the natural forces of the planet, these define our "unity in essentials." Such perspectives form our mission in a world which desperately needs to "see" them and draw strength from them, beyond parochial and provincial limits too narrow to affirm and sustain a global world of life. Unitarians and to some extent Universalists have been "deconstructing" narrow religious boundaries for two centuries. Now our gift to humanity is a perspective capable of holding the many strands in a wider and critical embrace. See Chapter Four.

22. John Lukacs, *Democracy and Populism*, (New Haven: Yale University Press, 2005), p. 30.

23. William Irwin Thompson, *Transforming History: A Curriculum for Cultural, Evolution*, (Great Barrington: Lindisfarne Books, 2001), pp. 78-81. See also Thompson's *The American Replacement of Nature*, (New York: Doubleday, 1991).

24. Edwin H. Friedman, *A Failure of Nerve: Leadership In the Age of the Quick Fix*, (Bethesda: Edwin Friedman Estate Trust, 1999), pp. 73-126.

25. John Lukacs, *The Passing of the Modern Age*, (New York: Harper, 1970),

p. 47.

26. Lee Harris, *Civilization and Its Enemies: The Next Stage of History*, (New York: Free Press, 2004), pp. 205-206.

27. Ibid., p. 208.

28. Lukacs, pp. 17-73.

29. Harris, pp. 49-67, 143-153.

30. Duncan Howlett, *The Fatal Flaw: At the Heart of Religious Liberalism*, (Amherst, NY: Prometheus Books, 1995), pp. 49-59.

31. Harris, p. 218.

32. Thompson, *The American Replacement of Nature*, pp. 29, 31, 70-71, 113, 150.

33. Ibid., p. 31.

34. The same threefold model developed here can be applied to social justice and service projects for congregations: (1) some will be determined by the congregational meeting as official congregation-wide commitments; (2) others will be projects or involvements by individuals; (3) still others will be ongoing projects of groups within the congregation.

CHAPTER THREE

1. Perry Miller (ed.), *Margaret Fuller American Romantic: A Selection from her Writings and Correspondence*, (New York: Anchor Books, 1963), p. 195.

2. Charles Grady, *Arlington's First Parish: A History, 1733-1990*, (Arlington: First Parish. 2000), pp. 35-48. and Douglas H. MacDonald, "A Theological History, 1835-1879, of the Bangor Unitarian Society." Mimeographed.

3. A withering critique of Hegel's view of history can be found in Bertrand Russell, *A History of Western Philosophy*, (New York: Simon and Schuster, 1945), pp. 730-746.

4. George H. Williams, "Rethinking the Unitarian Relationship with Protestantism: An Examination of the Thought of Frederic Henry

Hedge." *The Unitarian Universalist Christian*, Spring/Summer 1981, 36:1-2.

5. Rabindranath Tagore, "Historicality in Literature," in Ranajit Guha, *History at the Limit of World-History*, (New York: Columbia University Press, 2000), pp. 95-99.

6. Ralph Waldo Emerson, "Self-Reliance." *Essays: First Series*. Heritage Edition. p. 35.

7. Theodore Parker, *Experience as a Minister, with Some Account of his Early Life, and Education for the Ministry; Contained in a Letter from him to the Members of the Twenty-Eighth Congregational Society of Boston*, (Boston: Rufus Leighton, 1859). p. 81.

8. Perry Miller (ed.), Op. Cit., p. xi.

9. Ibid. p. 128.

10. From the oral traditions of Concord, MA (c/o Eleanor Richardson).

11. Odell Shepard (ed.), *The Heart of Thoreau's Journals*, (New York: Dover, 1961). pp. 6-7.

12. Henry David Thoreau, *Walden*, Heritage Edition. p. 317.

13. Shepard (ed.), Op. Cit., p. 124.

14. Conrad Wright, ed., *Three Prophets of Religious Liberalism: Channing-Emerson-Parker*, Boston: Beacon Press, 1961. p. 26.

15. Ralph Waldo Emerson, "The Divinity School Address," in Conrad Wright, p. 98. Reference is to Wordsworth's poem, "The World Is Too Much With Us.'

> Great God! I'd rather be
> A Pagan suckled in a creed outworn;
> So might I, standing on this pleasant lea,
> Have glimpses that would make me less forlorn;
> Have sight of Proteus rising from the sea;
> Or hear old Triton blow his wreathèd horn.

16. Two excellent articles develop the characteristics of Philosophia and the issues surrounding the idea. See Wilfred C. Smith, "Philosophia As One of the Religious Traditions of Humankind," in *Modern Culture*

from a Comparative Perspective, Albany: State University of New York Press, 1997; and Huston Smith, "Western Philosophy as a Great Religion," in *Essays on World Religion*. New York: Paragon House, 1995.

17. Wilfred Smith makes the critical observation that in the West uniquely people have their religion, Christianity, Judaism or Islam. In most branches of human culture you are born in a religion and simply are what you are. This virtually makes Philosophia invisible for it is the religion here we are born into, the "rationalist-idealist-humanist" complex. He credits his global perspective with his ability to recognize Philosophia for what it is. He speaks of religious complexes in various places such as the Far East where one is not a Confucian, Taoist, Animist, Buddhist, or Shinto for a person is not asked to opt out of one in order to "join" another as in Christianity or Islam. You have to look at how lives are affected by the religion. Philosophia involves the love of wisdom as well as the intellectual qualities of the Greek inheritance. Huston Smith's essay is best read after Wilfred Smith's. He both supports the idea of Philosophia enshrining it as one of the seven major religious complexes but limits it to the older prescientific strands of Western tradition. He adds important criteria for defining or setting aside Philosophia as a religion: communal, cultic, sense of ultimacy, a total involvement, theophanies, and ontology. He speaks of an intuitive authority for religion, a jnanic basis, which I have identified as intuitive thinking (NT), or the "Journey of Unity" in my *Four Spiritualities*. There is indeed an academic bias in both these presentations weighed towards the jnanic. There is little in their presentation for the "Journey of Devotion" (SF), which could be mined in the Roman practices of Stoicism and in the comprehensive matrix of the older pagan piety of the Greek, Etruscan, Celtic, Germanic and Scandinavian pre-Christian practices.

18. Ralph Waldo Emerson, "History." *Essays: First Series*, Heritage Edition, p. 5.

19. Emerson, "Self-Reliance." *Essays: First Series*, Heritage Edition, p. 36.

20. A high profile example may be Forrest Church, "Emerson's Shadow," *UU World*, XVII: 2, March/April 2003, pp. 29-31. This was the *World's* "Emerson at 200" issue.

21. Edwin H. Friedman, *Generation to Generation*, (New York: Guilford

Press, 1985). Also his posthumous book, A Failure of Nerve, (Bethesda, 1999). A fine video, *Reinventing Leadership*, (New York: Guilford Press, 1996), includes a discussion guide outlining Friedman's key ideas.

22. Robert Kegan's theory as it relates to an interpretation of Unitarian history is found in *The Boston Religion*, pp. 140, 220-222. The best source for his theory is still *In Over Our Heads*, (Cambridge: Harvard University Press, 1994). See also *How the Way We Talk Can Change the Way We Work*, (San Francisco: Jossey-Bass, 2001). It must be asked if a congregation of people in the third order can tolerate the challenges of those in the fourth order among them, or even if fourth order groups can agree to have an ideological diversity. And can a congregation mostly in the fourth order who require a high definition in their leaders (such as Friedman recommends) tolerate a fifth order leader who appears to be in many places and requires of them that they negotiate out their aspirations. And of course, can we prepare ways to hold people in the several orders of development so that they are supported in the present while we challenge them to grow further? Can a congregation encourage the presence of several orders in the same congregation, and have an effective congregational life without chaotic implosions from time to time? Perhaps as at present, those in the third will drift away to more comfortable surroundings that are supportive, and those in the fifth (or fourth/fifth), like Emerson, may have to exit with a mission to save their own souls, connected but apart. Spiritual growth is not a dabbling in this or that "practice," now this, now that, but rather is a growth in ability to enter into living at more degrees of complexity, to be able to function with poise and effectiveness, and after transitioning from the traditional third order, at greater capacities to bring the world inside to become centered (or multi-centered) and self-transforming there.

23. Emerson, "Compensation" *Essays: First Series*, Heritage Edition, p. 50.

24. Emerson, "Spiritual Laws" *Essays: First Series*, Heritage Edition, p. 56.

25. Emerson, "Oversoul," *Essays: First Series*, Heritage Edition, p. 108.

26. At age eight his father died and he outlived all seven siblings, several of whom at an early age he perceived as far more promising of success than he. The death of his first wife, Ellen, was devastating, relived in a sense by the death of his oldest son, Waldo. He saw his oldest brother

broken in spirit at a young age, helped support his younger brother who lived out his days developmentally disabled, made space in his home for a younger brother, Charles, who died before he could move in. Then of course he experienced a major vocational crisis in his youth, precipitating his move to Concord and his new life as lecturer, essayist and poet.

27. Van Wyck Brooks, *The Flowering of New England*, (New York: E. P. Dutton), 1957, p. 214. Jung's term is "the collective unconscious." Brooks refers the reader to Jung's *Modern Man in Search of a Soul*, a good choice. For an analysis of Jung's significance for social interpretation, see Ira Progoff, Jung's *Psychology and its Social Meaning*, (New York: Grove Press, 1953).

28. For a development of this view of Emerson see my *Four Spiritualities*, (Palo Alto: Davies-Black, 1996), pp. 146-148. The chapter, "Journey of Harmony," pp. 143-179, develops the nature of intuitive feeling spirituality.

29. 29. Emerson, "Nature," *Essays: Second Series*, Heritage Edition. PP. 224-225. There is much speculation as to the compatibility of Emerson's views of nature always unfolding, and the developments after Darwin's *Origin of Species* in 1860. Robert Richardson (p. 546) sees them as wholly compatible. Toulouse and Duke, in *Makers of Christian Theology In America*, while they see Emerson as beyond the pale of Christianity, do find his work as anticipating both pragmatism and process theology. Transcendentalism was really more an immanentalism, not lending itself to a scientific Theism such as we find in the next generation illustrated prominently by Minot Savage in Boston. Rather Emerson's immanental view of the energies and processes of nature, the spiritual arising in the stuff of nature, might lend itself creatively to the present explorations of cognitive psychology, a nondualistic view of the spiritual seen as ontological metaphor. See Lakoff and Johnson, *Philosophy In The Flesh* (1999) and *Metaphors We Live By* (1980). Emerson's opposition to empiricism was an opposition to externals, second hand spirituality. The new empiricism of embodiment is immanental, its ground within the individual. How this interface is understood may be the most critical work of Unitarian Universalist theology going forward.

30. R. Buckminster Fuller, *Synergetics*, (New York: MacMillan, 1975, 1979), 2 vols. This requires mathematical facility for understanding. I recommend his *Operating Manual for Spaceship Earth and Critical Path* as best for introductions to Fuller's thought. His *Utopia or Oblivion* is an excellent collection of his essays, *Ideas and Integrities* is quite autobiographical and introduces how he went about inventing in such a wide range, *Nine Chains to the Moon* is his earliest work and with theological observations as is found in his later *No More Secondhand God* and the poem *Intuition*. The most insightful biography of Fuller I have found to be E. J. Applewhite's *Cosmic Fishing*.

31. Quoted in E. J. Applewhite, *Cosmic Fishing*, (New York: MacMillan, 1977), p. 146.

32. Fuller, *No More Secondhand God*, (Carbondale: Southern Illinois University Press, 1963), p. 35. His report of his bridge experience can be found in Fuller, *Ideas and Integrities*, (New York: MacMillan, 1963), p. 45.

33. Quoted in Robert D. Richardson, *Emerson: The Mind on Fire*, (Berkeley: University of California Press, 1995), pp. 126-127.

34. Applewhite, p. 152.

CHAPTER FOUR

1. Ralph Waldo Emerson, "The Poet," *Essays: Second Series*, Heritage Edition, p. 165.

2. Joseph Priestley, *A Comparison of the Institutions of Moses with Those of the Hindoos and Other Ancient Nations*. (Northumberland: A. Kennedy, 1799), pp. 2-3.

3. Herrlee G. Creel, *Confucius and the Chinese Way*. (New York: Harper & Brothers, 1949), pp. 257, 261.

4. Samuel Longfellow, *Essays and Sermons*. (Boston: Houghton, Mifflin, 1894), pp. 70, 72.

5. Samuel Johnson, "Life of Ages" #111 in *Singing the Living Tradition*. (Boston: Beacon Press, 1993).

6. Samuel Johnson, *Oriental Religions and Their Relation to Universal Religion: India*. (Boston: James R. Osgood, 1873), p. 2.

7. Howard N. Meyer (ed.), *The Magnificent Activist: The Writings of Thomas Wentworth Higginson*. (DaCapo Press, 2000), p. 355.

8. Octavius Brooks Frothingham, "The Religion of Humanity" in *Proceedings at the Annual Meeting of the Free Religious Association*. 1872, p. 65.

9. Cited by Charles W. Wendte, "Address," *Proceedings at the Forty-Seventh Annual Meeting*. (Boston: Free Religious Association, 1914), p. 33.

10. Jenkin Lloyd Jones, "Closing Address," *Proceedings of the 26th Annual Meeting of the Free Religious Association*, 1893, p. 79. Speaking to the F.R.A. Jones said: "this Association was probably the spiritual seed that more than anything else gave rise to this great harvest field you call the Parliament of Religions."

11. William J. Potter, "The World's Parliament of Religions: Its Significance and Possible Results," in *Lectures and Sermons*. (Boston: George H. Ellis, 1895), p. 201. There were various views of what that new religion would be, for example the divergence of Minot Savage from Potter. See Richardson, p. 162.

12. Edmund C. Stedman, *Octavius Brooks Frothingham and the New Faith*. (New York: G. P. Putnam's Sons, 1876), p. 11.

13. Carl T. Jackson, *The Oriental Religions and American Thought: Nineteenth-Century Explorations*. (Westport: Greenwood Press, 1981), pp. 66, 134.

14. James Freeman Clarke, *Ten Great Religions*, (Boston: Houghton, Mifflin, 1886), frontispiece.

15. Leigh Eric Schmidt, *Restless Souls: The Making of American Spirituality*. (New York: Harper Collins, 2005), p. 183. See also Carl T. Jackson, *The Oriental Religions and American Thought: Nineteenth-Century Explorations*, and John B. Buescher, *The Other Side of Salvation*, (Boston: Skinner House, 2004.). Leigh's book documents how phase two responses to world religion moved beyond Unitarian bounds but with many Unitarian, particularly latter day Transcendentalist, participants, alongside parallel movements, Vedantic, Theosophical, Whitmanite, Bahá'í. The owner and patron of Greenacre for example

converted to the Bahá'í Faith. The Bahá'í belief in progressive revelation limits it to monotheistic, really Abrahamic, traditions. One Vedantic participant, Aldous Huxley, is mentioned with his *Perennial Philosophy*. This too limits a global embrace to certain theistic orientations. An advantage of humanistic, naturalistic orientations makes it possible to embrace theistic traditions as well since all are manifestations of the human spirit. It is possible to see our human nature in the faces of the gods/goddesses, even to remain ambiguous as to where the line between humanistic and theistic orientations may be drawn if indeed it is possible.

16. For example in the closing paragraph: "What man has made, man can make again. He has created many a spiritual world in the past, and he can build more stately mansions for the soul in the years to come. The old creations were visionary, largely unreal, of the substance of dreams, shot through with nightmare visions; but the newer realms of the spirit will be finer, with sounder basic foundations in human nature, and with loftier possibilities for the advancing of all human interests. Religion, therefore is not passing away, but coming into its own." This naïve view of the passing of the traditional and substitution of the new came not from nineteenth century theism but from twentieth century sociology. George Willis Cooke, *The Social Evolution of Religion*, (Boston: The Stratford Company, 1920), p. 402.

17. Louis C. Cornish, "International Relations of the American Unitarian Association," in *Unitarians Face a New Age*. (Boston: Commission of Appraisal, 1936), p. 116.

18. Curtis W. Reese, ed., *Humanist Sermons*, (Chicago: Open Court, 1927), p. 253.

19. John H. Dietrich, *Humanism*, (Boston: American Unitarian Association, 1933), p. 21.

20. Sunday Program, "The Community Church of Boston (Non-Sectarian) Symphony Hall," Sunday, January 11, 1942, p. 1.

21. See my *The Boston Religion*, pp. 131-142, for a history of the Charles Street Meeting House in Boston.

22. A. Eustace Haydon, *Man's Search for the Good Life*. (New York: Harper & Brothers, 1937), p. 82.

23. Kenneth L. Patton, *A Religion for One World*, (Boston: Meeting House Press and Beacon Press, 1964), p. 125.

23. Kenneth L. Patton, *The Chinese Poets of Nature and Humanity*, (Ridgewood: Meeting House Press, 1984), p. xxxvii.

25. Kenneth L. Patton (ed.), *The Way for This Journey*, (Ridgewood: Meeting House Press, 1976), p. vii.

26. Patton, *A Religion for One World*, p. 126.

27. Kenneth L. Patton, *Kaggen, The Mantis: Folklore of the Cape Bushmen*, (Ridgewood: Meeting House Press, c. 1980), p. xi.

28. Ibid., p. 115.

29. Donald Szantho Harrington, *Unitarian Universalism Yesterday, Today and Tomorrow*: a Sermon preached on the occasion of the celebration of the consolidation of The American Unitarian Association and The Universalist Church of America. Boston, May 23, 1960, p. 15. Harrington's overall view was more in the tradition of phase two than phase three. However, both agree in the importance of interfaith families in our midst.

30. Floyd H. Ross et al, "World Religion and Outreach" in *The Free Church in a Changing World*, (Boston: Unitarian Universalist Association, 1993), pp. 132-155.

31. Spencer Lavan, ed., *Unitarian Universalist Views of World Religions*, (Boston: Unitarian Universalist Association), p. 10. A recent study by Tomoko Masuzawa, confirms Patton's historical insight. See her *The Invention of World Religions*, (Chicago: University of Chicago Press, 2005).

32. *Report of the Committee on Goals*, Boston: Unitarian Universalist Association, 1967, p. 37.

33. Were I to write such a line at a microphone today I would drop the "s" in the word, religions, or substitute for religions, "religious traditions."

34. A symptom of this need is evidenced by a report issued the spring of 2005: Commission On Appraisal, *Engaging Our Theological Diversity*. (Boston: Unitarian Universalist Association, 2005), 177 pp. I wrote a

critique of this report reflecting the perspective outlined in Lecture Four which follows in part here:

...Indeed "interreligious dialogue" seemed to be furthest from their intention, and they made every effort to discourage it. They set the table but brought no food. There was a strange quote from a Methodist scholar, Huston Smith, warning us off "cafeteria-style spirituality" as an exercise for what he called "Saint Ego" which I took to be something like Jung's concept of the inflated ego. Why the two would be necessarily linked is a mystery to me and the Commission made no effort to explain.

They did go to further lengths however to discourage exploration of our world religious inheritance. Immediately after the Smith quote is their summary:

Other traditions should not be used as distractions from Unitarian Universalism's own path.

Aside from the assertion that "other" traditions are employed to distract, they engage in what they warn us against, turning to Protestant Christian authorities for the most part to critique our own path, in one instance as an expert consultant. This proclivity to use the word "other," as in "other religions," is repeated (pp. 89-90, 147, 150) without clear guidance for what they consider not to be "other." It would appear to be Protestant Christianity of the mainstream sort particularly positioned in academia with passing mention of UU Buddhists, UU Pagans, UUs for Jewish Awareness, UU Christians, the UU Process Theology Network, and UU humanists.

We are warned repeatedly against "this exotic fashionability of non-Judeo-Christian sources." (p. 88) Indeed "this exoticism" is seen by the Commission to be largely "tokenizing" and even "racist." Tokenizing is defined as "selectively picking and choosing." (p. 88) Isn't this what any systematic approach to theology is supposed to do? Is any choosing of a non European, or more exactly non Euro-North American-Protestant, content necessarily an exercise of "white power." This absurd assertion is an undercurrent throughout the report as if a reading of the Bhagavad-Gita or the Chuang-tzu is necessarily "exotic" and "racist." Woe to all our forebears who did so: Joseph Priestley, Ralph Waldo Emerson, H. D. Thoreau, T. Parker, Samuel Longfellow, Samuel Johnson, Thomas W. Higginson, J. F. Clarke, Jenkin L. Jones, Octavius

B. Frothingham, Clarence Skinner, Kenneth Patton and countless others in "our own" tradition! Perhaps they were all racists without knowing it. The notion that only a part of our human inheritance on this planet is legitimate and the rest "exotic" and if chosen, "racist," is absurd in the context of the early twenty-first century. Indeed this argument could be reversed. Would it not be racist to confine one's attentions only to white Christian sources? Commission members it seems know just enough of post-modern deconstructionism to be dangerous.

We are warned repeatedly by the Commission against "misappropriation," while they go on to use the term "Judeo-Christianity" in five instances. This linkage is not appreciated by most Jews, seen by them as an effort by Christians to subordinate and assimilate the unique features of their tradition. A response to the issue of "misappropriation" is to acknowledge that it happens all the time, both within and from outside all traditions of human religion. Was it not our own Joseph Priestley who wrote *A History of the Corruptions of Christianity?* Priestley went on to write *A Comparison of the Institutions of Moses with Those of the Hindoos and Other Ancient Nations* published in 1799. That misappropriation happens is no excuse for withdrawing one's boundaries into an insular parochialism! All this warning may accomplish is to discourage the intellectually timid and apathetic from mustering an attempt to connect with their rich inheritance in our human religious past.

In addition it is from "misappropriation" that new religious impulses are born: witness Roman Catholic and Greek Orthodox Christianity, Mohammed's Islam, Vedantic forms of Hinduism, the sublime traditions of the goddess Kuan Yin in China. In the realm of music where would jazz or the blues be without repeated "misappropriations?" The time has come for well meaning liberals to refrain from barging into the defense of local traditions around the world and to leave the preservation of the purity of these enclaves to their own practitioners who are far more capable of getting it "right" anyway.

The Commission does include several positive vignettes, for example a section on "Hospitality" (pp. 119-122). They point out that all traditions share an affirmation of hospitality as a religious practice. They quote Sister Chittister that this is a "first step toward dismantling the barriers of the world." In the Benedictine tradition one may "joyfully make room for another inside your open heart." *Isaiah* and Howard Thurman are also cited as supporting Hospitality. Such attitudes are reinforced by a fine quote of a Tibetan greeting, "And to what sublime tradition do you belong?" (p. 150) I wish from this base the Commission had suggested systematic strategies for a global embrace based in personal and communal "hospitality."

One of the Commission's recommendations is to "Affirm Cultural Competency." (pp. 149-150) The assumption here seems to be that there are many cultures around the globe and that all are in some ways alien to each other. An alternative analysis would be that culture is a product of our human nature, indeed a defining characteristic of what it is to be human, one human culture with many branches. In relating to the diversity in our global cultural environment we grow in our humanity just as in a family relationship we grow to our maturity. To the extent that we see others as always "other" we fail to profit from our kinship. To be in friendly "dialogue," even hospitable, at arms length is quite different than the experience of a mutual participation for a global plenitude.

Even here the Commission closes down what energy it may be encouraging for a full bodied hospitality. In a discussion of "Depth versus Breath," the assumption being that if you have one you cannot have the other, the Commission advocates a deferring to the experts. One must become specialized. "Spirituality is not academics, but something similar is true of it." (p. 89) This is expertism, the idea that one cannot expand one's horizons without becoming an expert in each new realm. Spirituality it appears is being treated like pieces of knowledge, or new items for one's bag of tricks, rather than an inner process of development whereby appropriate aspects of our global religious inheritance are chosen and forged in the fires of unique experience. No wonder it has become common for UUs to "hyphenate" their religious identity. Such timid deference or even intimidation by expertism contradicts a fine quote from UU minister Fred Muir (p. 55): "Diversity means embracing otherness and, in so doing, becoming whole."

It is time for our supposed UU "pluralism" to enter a more mature phase. For one thing I categorically oppose the sentence (p. 90), "Perhaps if we had more to offer within Unitarian Universalism, they might not feel such a need to go elsewhere." Rather it is time for us to practice generosity, to encourage and support our people into participation in larger religious experiences, and as religious communities to welcome back new learnings and reports to enrich all. The old model of insularity, competition with surrounding religions, "converting" (pp. 35, 41, 87), must be discarded. Particularly as our congregations learn to welcome their interfaith families, becoming multifaith in composition, our pluralism must deepen in its generosity for the development of each member, not seeking to confine them to a common ("UUism") mold. The discussion of "marking boundaries" (p. 12) must take into consideration this communal generosity set in a new model of our mission in the world, to become in microcosm what we expect of world society. The Commission cited Diana Eck's observation that America is "the world's most religiously diverse nation." A mature UU pluralism will see this environment as a remarkable resource and opportunity to serve the world through becoming what the world may yet become.

Three references in the report are regrettable. The terms "universal church" (p. 21) and "The 'new world religion' Universalists" (p. 144) are highly misleading, particularly when the only reference to Kenneth Patton (p. 90) is dropped into the text without any context for who he was and what views he espoused. While in earlier generations with the Free Religious Association and their allies in the nineteenth and early twentieth century these terms, as phrased here, would have been appropriate, by the mid twentieth century a perspective had developed beyond the idea of creating "a new world religion" or "a universal church" to the concept of *A Religion for One World* or a religion capable of embracing and serving a global humanity. Unfortunately by commission or by omission the report falls into this misunderstanding.

One of the Commission's recommendations is that we "Make Peace with Our Religious Past." I wish that they had given us a list of theological sources from that past so that we would have a clear idea of what they have in mind. Instead they issued another warning against "exoticism," as if that might consist in "denying our roots." They complain of a proclivity in some quarters for a reactivity to Christianity. But the issue is not one of either/or. This new movement they have identified as "exoticism" it is claimed "leads to an uncritical acceptance of other[sic], less familiar traditions such as Buddhism or Hinduism." (p. 147) We thus have "reactivity" to Christianity and we have "exoticism" as hindrances to affirmation of "our own religious past." Of course a global embrace will include Christianity and cannot be accomplished without it.

Within an easy commute of many of our congregations are some of the world's great museums. I recommend making a special effort to visit the "exotic" galleries. Seeing the human image in many local traditions, the beautiful with the ugly, the true with the false, the good with the evil, may assuage glib condemnations of "exoticism" be they images Christian, Buddhist, Chinese or Native American. Likewise an excursion in the world's scriptures and spiritual writings will not break down into "exotic" versus "ours" whatever "ours" may be. Are the world's poets only writing for Europe, or for Persia, or for China? No, they address our humanity.

35. Huntington's list of "civilizations" seems arbitrary. He considers civilization a more inclusive term than "cultural groups." If civilizations hold together the cultural matrices in which people live then how can he justify his fault line theory, that there are permanent fault lines between civilizations. Huntington counters the whole drama of human emergence on the planet and six thousand years of history recording the interdependence and mutuality of influence among the branches of human culture. Indeed Lee Harris in his *Civilization and Its Enemies*, makes what I believe to be a more correct distinction between culture and civilization, the latter having universal characteristics which can be evaluated and graded with the former holding diverse local variations. In this context his main criticism of Huntington is his naiveté in believing that the "west" is alone in seeking to impose a "superior" mission on others. Not only have influences always flowed around the globe among cultural centers, but often defeated peoples manage to profoundly influence those who conquer. The conquered often conquer.

Were Huntington's thesis accurate the most basic understandings of human nature as universal, for example perspectives of Jungian psychology and psychological type as the differentiation of human consciousness (about which I have written elsewhere) would be called into question. It is true that the content and even orientations of enculturation in the various branches of culture is quite different. For example the differences between Western and Far Eastern thinking are illustrated by Richard Nisbett in his *The Geography of Thought* and by two outstanding translations of the Chinese classics with fine introductions, one by Ames and Rosemont, *The Analects of Confucius* and the other by Ames and Hall, *The DaodeJing*. Diversity among human centers is creative and gives us perspectives on our shared human nature. But we are one species, not permanent aliens to each other, and the long view makes us one culture with many family variations as well. For example, for a discussion of our inborn language faculty and what Noam Chomsky calls the human "Universal Grammar" see his *On Nature and Language*. Experiments have been conducted where people widely distributed around the globe have been asked "to read" photographed expressions on faces in very different cultural locations: expressions of anger, terror, joy, grief, happiness, etc. (an exercise of the Jungian function, Sensing). The accuracy of these "readings" is universal.

In addition Lee Harris in *Civilization and Its Enemies* makes an important distinction between what he calls "team cosmopolitanism" and what he identifies as the traditional "liberal cosmopolitanism." The latter has collapsed primarily because not all parties on the world scene agree to play by the same rules. It has no conceptual way to deal with destructive or ruthless forms of "self determination." He proposes a "team cosmopolitanism" where standards of civilized behavior and relationship can be advanced and enforced always with the restraints of a code of honor prohibiting exploitation and empire. He further insists that world community cannot be in the abstract but must be locally experienced. His perspective gives us a powerful argument for the working through of a global consciousness as the great task of congregational life, tested in the fires of that communal participation, as a model for world well-being and the preparation of individuals to participate in that world.

36. Peter T. Richardson, *Growing Your Spirituality*. (Rockland: Red Barn Publishing, 2001), pp. 109-121. *Archetype of the Spirit* will be published soon.

37. See *The Boston Religion*, pp. 220-222. Parallel to Robert Kegan's third, fourth and fifth orders of consciousness (see *In Over Our Heads*) I would propose three orders of interfaith/multifaith relationship. Each of these orders of consciousness as defined by Kegan are found in Unitarian Universalist congregations and thus it is imperative to

address them living side by side in community. In a multifaith congregation therefore the most basic system will be these three orders with an overlay of how those from very different traditions of origin will come to understand each other.

Tolerance, a "live and let live" attitude, runs parallel with Kegan's third order. In human society tolerance is an achievement not to be underrated. Fortunately in a society such as the United States it is written into the social contract with the Bill of Rights and other working understandings. The norm is a religious pluralism (still requiring some vigilance to maintain). In congregational life to cultivate an hospitable environment, including in worship, educational and social projects, elements from each tradition present and even anticipating those that might be present at some future time, is an enlightened generosity of spirit. As Kegan's third order of consciousness is the prevailing mainstream orientation in human society, and with continuing deference to social authorities a perfectly complete way of living a good life, there should be no inference that the attitude of tolerance is in some way inferior or incomplete. Support for this order should at least equal any coaxing or nudging of individuals toward the next order of complexity. Any transition is an organic, often painful (therefore needing support and reassurance), and incrementally unperceivable process.

If the third order is the traditionalist or socialized mind where tolerance is the way to relate to diversity, the fourth order is the autonomous or modern mind where choices and decisions become internalized and individual. Once conflicting social values and imperatives can be resolved within, then from this base dialogue with alternatives becomes possible. In a sense, dialogue is arms-length like tolerance; we can understand the other person(s) bringing in insights without stressing ourselves out, and we can enrich our own orientation through dialogue but we still have our own ground from which to engage the world. We are self creating, self determining, independent in our judgments and negotiations.

There comes a time for some when a single center of self becomes unsatisfactory, not in an experience of rejecting it but rather that parallel centers constellate until one's ground is multifarious. Spiritually this development can be characterized as a global consciousness, a condition of being at home in the many branches of human religion (in varying degrees). A person in a global consciousness affirms a global loyalty and participation, a universalism rather than a partialism. Social actions for justice, expressed ideals, reported life experience come from this world perspective. In any local religious community this orientation can be off putting in the same sense as Margaret Fuller's description of Ralph Waldo Emerson portrays, quoted at the beginning of Chapter Three. Many in the fourth order expect one to make common cause in an ideological stance and third order traditionalists expect a reinforcing of their values and life roles and expectations. Thus fifth order religious leaders and participants can be perceived as aloof or ambiguous or even weak in their supportiveness and commitments.

When a religious community is able to support and gain an active participation from all three orders (3-5), avoiding periodic implosions, with the responses of tolerance, dialogue and a global consciousness present and active, all benefit. There is immediate connection in a more perceptive way for strategies to leaven the general (traditionalist) population which surrounds any congregation. On the other hand there will be strongly motivated change agents among the fourth order members, introducing new ideas and reforms made more insightful with the ongoing practice of dialogue. And this group as well, if they are intentionally receptive, will be exposed to broader and deeper perspectives framing narrower passions and too predictable ("liberal") reactivity in society with appreciation of ways (conceptualizations) in which adversarial positions are embraced in shared assumptions and that beyond these assumptions yet more can be found releasing deadlocks and myopic anticipations of win or lose futures.

38. Peter T. Richardson, *Four Spiritualities*. Here I developed a theory describing four parallel ways of being and doing spirituality, found within and among the branches of human religious culture around the world. These four are (1) the Journey of Unity, (2) the Journey of Devotion, (3) the Journey of Works, and (4) the Journey of Harmony. For example, in India you would find the Buddha as an example of the Journey of Unity, Ramakrishna an example for the Journey of Devotion, Gandhi an example for the Journey of Works, and Tagore or Kabir as examples of the Journey of Harmony. The four schools of Yoga, Jnana, Bhakti, Karma, and Raja respectively, closely parallel the Four Spiritualities. In the western branch of religious culture you could place Socrates, Mohammed, Moses and Jesus respectively for the four.

In China there is a profound dialectic of Confucian teachers (Journey of Works) and the Taoist sages (Journey of Harmony) with imported Buddhist elements amply filling the remaining two. Bodhidharma represents well the Journey of Unity and Mo Tzu is an ancient apologist for the Journey of Devotion. The Four Spiritualities correlate with the differentiation of consciousness as described in Jungian psychological typology. Intuitive Thinking (NT) correlates with Unity, Sensing Feeling (SF) correlates with Devotion, Sensing Thinking (ST) correlates with Works, and Intuitive Feeling (NF) correlates with Harmony. These four orientations of human spirituality and consciousness are archetypal, present at the origins of the major clusters of religion as they emerged with the advent of written scriptures and traditions. A sequel work, *Archetype of the Spirit*, soon to be published, describes this archetypal complex.

39. Henry Rosemont, Jr., *Rationality and Religious Experience: the Continuing Relevance of the World's Spiritual Traditions*, (Chicago: Open Court, 2001), p. 89.

40. Ranajit Guha, *History at the Limit of World-History*, (New York: Columbia University Press, 2002), pp. 78-79.

41. Michael Polanyi, *The Tacit Dimension*, (New York: Anchor Books, 1966), p. 90.

42. Muhammad Asad, *The Road to Mecca*, (New York: Simon and Schuster, 1954), p. 395.

For Further Reading

THIS VOLUME OF COURSE STANDS UPON THE STORY narrated in *The Boston Religion: Unitarianism in Its Capital City*. Its churches and numerous leaders both characterized and impacted the emergence and development of the American Unitarian movement and to a major degree American culture as well.

The list below I consider as central for the libraries and reading of Unitarian Universalist ministers and leaders for understanding the Unitarian side of our living tradition.

CLASSIC SOURCES

William Ellery Channing, *Works*, 6 vols. Particularly "Likeness to God," "Unitarian Christianity," "Remarks On Associations," "Spiritual Freedom," "Self-Culture."
Ralph Waldo Emerson, *Essays*, Particularly "Self-Reliance," and "The Poet."
Octavius Brooks Frothingham, *Boston Unitarianism*, 1890.
Theodore Parker, *Experience as a Minister*, 1859.
Kenneth L. Patton, *A Religion for One World*, 1964.
Curtis W. Reese, ed., *Humanist Sermons*, 1927.
Henry David Thoreau, *Walden*.

OTHER SOURCES

Charles W. Akers, *Called Unto Liberty: A Life of Jonathan Mayhew*, (Cambridge: Harvard University Press, 1964).
Arthur S. Bolster, *James Freeman Clarke*, (Boston: Beacon Press, 1954).
Van Wyck Brooks, *The Flowering of New England*, (New York: Dutton, 1936).
George W. Cooke, *Unitarianism in America*, (Boston: A.U.A., 1902)

Ann Douglas, *The Feminization of American Culture*, (New York: Knopf, 1977).

Mark W. Harris, *Historical Dictionary of Unitarian Universalism*, (Lanham, Md: Scarecrow, 2004).

Daniel W. Howe, *The Unitarian Conscience*, (Cambridge: Harvard, 1970).

Duncan Howlett, *The Critical Way in Religion*, (Buffalo: Prometheus Books, 1980).

Carl T. Jackson, *The Oriental Religions and American Thought*, (Westport Ct.: Greenwood, 1981).

Charles H. Lippy, *Seasonable Revolutionary: The Mind of Charles Chauncy*, (Chicago: Nelson-Hall, 1981).

Jack Mendelsohn, *Channing: The Reluctant Radical*, (Boston: Little Brown, 1971).

Kenneth L. Patton, *Chinese Humanism*, (Ridgewood, NJ: Meeting House, c. 1985).

Kenneth L. Patton, *Man's Hidden Search*, (Boston: Meeting House, 1954).

Robert D. Richardson Jr., *Emerson: The Mind on Fire*, (Berkeley: California, 1995).

Leigh Eric Schmidt, *Restless Souls: The Making of American Spirituality*, (San Francisco: Harper, 2005).

Carl Scovel & Charles Forman, *Journey Toward Independence*, (Boston: Skinner, 1993).

Leonard Silk & Mark Silk, *The American Establishment*, 1980.

Conrad Wright, *The Beginnings of Unitarianism in America*, (Boston: Starr King, 1955).

Conrad Wright, *The Liberal Christians*, (Boston: Beacon, 1970).

Index

Other Books By the Author

The Boston Religion: Unitarianism In Its Capital City
Describes Unitarian history, theology, sociology and interface with
American culture, through the ministers and laity of Boston's 74
congregations. Hardbound, 264 pages, 139 illustrations, index.
Red Barn Publishing, 29.95.

Four Spiritualities: A Psychology of Contemporary Spiritual Choice
Correlates four parallel patterns found within all branches of human
religion with Jungian psychological type and the MBTI. Paperback, 245
pages, 10 illustrations, index, Davies-Black Publishing, $18.95.

*Growing Your Spirituality: A workshop and seminar guide for applying
Four Spiritualities to your life*
Typescript, bound, 166 pages, 8 illustrations. Red Barn Publishing,
$12.00.

Archetype of the Spirit
Through ancient motifs and symbols around the world, describes the
archetype for spiritual development and wholeness found on all continents. This is the archetype behind *Four Spiritualities* correlated with
psychological type. Illustrated, index. Available December 2006, *cost tba.*

TO ORDER the above or additional copies of *Exloring Unitarian
Universalist Identity* contact the author at Red Barn Publishing,
22 Mechanic Street, Rockland, ME 04841, 207-596-5502.
PTEMR@aol.com.

NOTE: Please add 3.50 p & h. Maine residents add 5 % sales tax.